Underneath This Smile

Based on
the blog,
Rebecca's
Challenge

REBECCA LEATHERWOOD

ISBN 978-1-68517-446-0 (paperback)
ISBN 978-1-68517-447-7 (digital)

Christian Faith Publishing
832 Park Avenue
Meadville, PA 16335
www.christianfaithpublishing.com

Printed in the United States of America

This book is dedicated in loving memory of
Bobby Leatherwood (November 24, 1935–April 7, 2021),
Marine, husband, father, Paw-paw.

Letter to the Reader

To my dear reader,

Before you read this book, there are few things I would like for you to know before you start. First of all, I would like to say thank you for getting my book and for taking the time to read it. I appreciate you! Now I want to tell you a little about the book you're reading because you need to know about these things before you start. This book was originally a blog called Rebecca's Challenge. I had a blog before I ever had books. Most of the blog entries that were written are in this book; however, there are a few that were left out on purpose because they were not appropriate for what I needed this book to be. I started my blog in 2015, and my last blog entry was written in 2019. What you are looking at is a compilation of all my original blog entries, which I have collected over the years.

I have turned my writings into a semi-interactive devotional. Some pages will have questions that I would like you to take the time to answer for yourself. There are no lines for you to write on because I want you to find your favorite journal and a good pen so that you can write your own thoughts down and answer the questions honestly. The journal you pick should be for your eyes only! I do not want someone to pick up this book or borrow it and have your personal thoughts exposed. That's why I recommend a separate journal. Some pages are just things I needed to write about and are for you to think about; you don't have to do anything. I hope that you also take the time to laugh. There is some funny stuff too!

All the dates at the top of the pages are the original dates of when I wrote the blog entries. All the titles are original as well. I like to be as authentic as possible!

As you walk through this book with me, I hope that not only will it touch your heart but also help you with some real issues that you might have. Most importantly, I hope that it can be used as an accessory in your walk with Christ. If you don't know Christ, I hope you come to know Him by the time you finish this book.

Everything I wrote is real, and you'll be walking though different seasons of my life.

Everyone is walking through life, but not everyone is bold enough to write about it and share it with the whole world. I laughed and cried my own tears while getting this ready for you.

If even one page changes the way you look at something in your own life, then it was worth it all to me.

Enjoy your book and know it's coming from my heart.

Sincerely,
Rebecca Leatherwood

The Word *Never*

May 31, 2015

Having cerebral palsy is something no one expects to have in their life. I have had this all my life, so I don't know how to live any differently. Growing up and even now, I hear the word *never*. The doctors told me I would never play sports, walk, or run, and that I would become nothing in life. Today, I have a black belt in karate, I have played soccer, and I have been able to teach special needs children. The word *never* does not exist in God's vocabulary. How many times do you let the word *never* get to you?

The words that come out of our mouths are powerful. The words we use for ourselves often describe what we really think about ourselves. If we think that we will never become anything or that we can never do something, we won't because our mind has already made the choice for us.

How many times have you let the word *never* stop you?

The Shortest and the Smallest

June 2, 2015

When I started school, I was the shortest and smallest, and I never talked. I never talked because I looked so different from the others, and the other kids did not want much to do with me. I guess they were having too much fun making jokes and staring at me. I am now nineteen years old, and I have had five major surgeries to make me look and feel better. Today, you can hardly tell anything was wrong at all.

Throughout my life, I have been able to keep a smile on my face. In life, we can meet some of the shortest, smallest, and quietest people. Most of the time, those are the ones who can teach you the most. They can even teach you how to smile no matter how much pain you're in.

> Better to hear the quiet words of a wise person than the shouts of a foolish king. (Ecclesiastes 9:17)

> If your boss is angry at you, don't quit! A quiet spirit can overcome even great mistakes. (Ecclesiastes 10:4)

> It is foolish to belittle one's neighbor; a sensible person keeps quiet. (Proverbs 11:12)

The Beauty of the Cross

June 5, 2015

Jesus knows everything about us before we are even born. He knows when we do good and when we sin. He knows when we are strong and when we are weak. That means He already knew I was going to have cerebral palsy. It also means He knew when I was going to be strong and when I was going to be weak. Jesus knows when I do good and when I sin. That is the beauty of the cross! Jesus died on the cross for the good, the bad, the weak, and the strong. Because of the cross, God has taken a little girl with cerebral palsy and made her strong. Because of the cross, He has taken all her sins to help her do good not for herself but for the *kingdom*! That does not mean I am not sad or weak at times; it's just that when I want to quit, someone comes along and makes me strong.

Jesus can do the same for you! You just have to ask *Him*!

O Lord, you have examined my heart and know everything about me. (Psalm 139:1)

You saw me before I was born. Every day of my life was recorded in your book. Every moment was laid out before a single day had passed. (Psalm 139:16)

What Can Children Do?

June 6, 2015

Ever since I can remember, I have loved caring for babies and toddlers, and as I got older, I loved helping preschoolers and kindergarteners. For most people, that seems like the hardest thing in the world, but for me, it seems like the only thing I did not have to work at. I love the little ones, and they love me too. For someone like me who always had older kids running away from her, little kids mean everything. Why the little kids? Little kids don't care what you look like. All they care about is how much time you spend with them and what activity is next. Babies like to be loved on and cared for. And toddlers can be rough, but they can also be some of the most loving people we have on this earth. For me to have a baby on my hip and a toddler running at me instead of away from me is one of the most healing things I could ever have. Children have the ability to heal if you just give them the chance.

That is what children can do!

If we are not careful, we may develop the thought that our children are burdens instead of blessings. We also tend to forget that our children are smaller than us and the world's problems. They are not made to carry our world on their shoulders.

They were made to shine in our lives at the darkest moments without us realizing it.

You just have to take the time to see it.

Your children are a gift from the *Lord*.

Children are a gift from the Lord; they are
a reward from him. (Psalm 127:3)

One day some parents brought their little children to Jesus so he could touch and bless them. But when the disciples saw this, they scolded the parents for bothering him. Then Jesus called for the children and said to the disciples, "Let the children come to me. Don't stop them! For the Kingdom of God belongs to those who are like these children. I tell you the truth, anyone who doesn't receive the Kingdom of God like a child will never enter it." (Luke 18:15–17)

Learning How to Walk

June 8, 2015

When I was little, learning how to walk was a challenge. I was not able to walk until I was three years old. Now that I'm nineteen, I have learned how to walk three times throughout my life. When you're learning how to walk, you fall *a lot*! There were so many times in my life that I had more bruises and busted knees than anything else. When I would try to get back up, it was never easy, and having braces on my legs did not make it any better. Somehow, I always managed to get back up. Most of the time, I could do it by myself, but sometimes I would need someone to hold my hand to help me get back up.

In life, we can go through really hard times and fall down. We always think we have to go through it by ourselves. You don't have to do it by yourself. Sometimes we need extra help or someone to hold our hand to help us get back up. Most of the time, the only reason we don't ask for help is because of our own pride, or we have been forced to be so independent that we don't know how to ask for help.

If you're reading this, you are in one of two places. You are either the person who has too much pride to ask for help and have developed the "I can do it all by myself, and I can do it better than you" attitude, or you are the person who has been forced to be independent because of life circumstances and really don't know how to ask for help. There is nothing wrong with wanting to be independent, but if it puts you in a position where you are fearful of asking for help, it will become a problem. Your problem may very well become someone else's opportunity to be a blessing.

> You want what you don't have, so you scheme and kill to get it. You are jealous of what others have, but you can't get it, so you fight and wage war to take it away from them. Yet you don't have what you want because you don't ask God for it. And even when you ask, you don't get it because your motives are all wrong you want only what will give you pleasure. (James 4:2–3)

> Pride leads to disgrace, but with humility comes wisdom. (Proverbs 11:2)

> Pride leads to conflict; those who take advice are wise. (Proverbs 13:10)

> Pride ends in humiliation, while humility brings honor. (Proverbs 29:23)

Success

June 10, 2015

People can define success in so many ways. Some might say you can find it in money, fame, what you do for a living, or how many possessions you may have. Success for me has to do with *none* of those things. Growing up, all I wanted was to walk, run, play sports, have real friends who loved me for who I was and not for who I was not able to be, make it through school, and do something extraordinary with my life that no one else could. God let me do all those things. There was a lot of pain in trying to accomplish all these things, but I did it. And it had nothing to do with money, my job, fame, or possessions! Today I can walk, run, and play sports, and I have the best friends I could ever ask for. And to be honest, they are more like my family. I would not trade the people God has given me for anything. I have even been able to do something extraordinary with my life. I have been able to defeat the odds in my life and go on mission trips to share God's love and His Word. I will always have cerebral palsy for a challenge, but I will never let it stop me. That is *success*!

If I were to ask you personally how you define success, what would you tell me?

> Study this Book of Instruction continually. Meditate on it day and night so you will be sure to obey everything written in it. Only then will you prosper and succeed in all you do. (Joshua 1:8)

> Seek his will in all you do, and he will show you which path to take. (Proverbs 3:6)

God's Mirror

June 12, 2015

I get so tired of the media, radio, magazines, and weight-loss commercials determining who or what we should look like. We are all made differently, and that is what makes us beautiful. Being made differently proves that God made us with His own hands. It breaks my heart to see girls and women looking in the mirror and feeling so bad about the way they look. I wish I could say I never struggled with self-image, but here is what made the difference: When I was twelve years old, someone told me I was made in the image of Christ and that there was a diamond in my heart just waiting to be shined. God took the diamond, buffed it, polished it, took out all the good, and let it shine. And after so many years of struggle, He made my body just like He wanted it to be.

Today I am confident that God made me. He made you too, and I know that He is not finished yet! Sometimes I want to buy the world a great big trash can and throw away the magazines, media, radio, and commercials. Go look in God's mirror and not yours, then tell me how beautiful you really are!

Dear women, I see you!
Dear young women, I hear your voice!
Dear teenage girl, I feel your pain inside and out!
Dear little girl, please don't ever forget that God made you!

For we are God's masterpiece. He has created us anew in Christ Jesus, so we can do the good things he planned for us long ago. (Ephesians 2:10)

Thank you for making me so wonderfully complex! Your workmanship is marvelous how well I know it. (Psalm 139:14)

Wounds Heal

June 15, 2015

Having so many surgeries and doctor visits can do something to a person. To this day, I don't believe the doctor when they say that it's not going to hurt because it always comes out to be the opposite. Surgery also causes you to have scars, which, most the time, leave permanent damage to your skin. Most of my scars are very easy to see, and there is a story behind every one. The best part about wounds is that they heal. In life, we can get hurt, and sometimes it will leave a scar and leave damage in your heart. When the wounds heal, you will have a story to tell about each one. And even though the scars are easy to see, you can use it to heal someone else's heart. Wounds heal to help heal!

You may not have physical scars on your body like I do, but you may have scars inside you, which no one else can see. It may be mental, emotional, or even spiritual. My question for you is this: Have you let those wounds heal properly? Even as a believer in Christ, I struggle with this because healing from something on the inside can feel like peeling off a Band-Aid very slowly. Healing may require tears, but remember, Jesus has cried with you and for you too.

> But he was pierced for our rebellion, crushed
> for our sins. He was beaten so we could be whole.
> He was whipped so we could be healed. (Isaiah
> 53:5)

The Quiet Ones

June 16, 2015

As I went through school, I was the student who sat in the back of the class and never talked. I never talked because I was so afraid of what the kids would say to me. As I got older, I found it easier to talk to adults, not just because I grew up around adults my whole life, but because I could relate to them better. In school, I was not the one who was book-smart. As I would talk to adults, they would begin to see that I was not just a crazy kid with no life skills. They would see that I actually had a lot of common sense and would tell me that I was wise beyond my years. I gained a lot of respect from adults because of my different outlook on life, and they saw that I could actually help them go through life instead of making it harder or just being in the way. I am "life-smart," which is better than book-smart because it keeps you out of trouble. Sometimes, the ones who are the most quiet are the ones who know the most, and sometimes, the ones who say the least are the ones who should be saying the most. You just have to take the time to listen.

> Don't let anyone thing less of you because you are young. Be an example to all believers in what you say, in the way you live, in your love, your faith, and your purity. (1 Timothy 49:3)

Labels

June 20, 2015

All too often, people label others. I was labeled throughout my life, and as I would change, my label would also change. People would not even remember my real name because of what the other kids would call me. My name was no longer Rebecca; I was labeled as the "girl who walks funny," "fat," and "the girl with braces." I remember getting so excited if someone remembered my name even if they turned it into a joke. Now that I have gotten a little older and had a "God makeover," I got my name back and have many other labels. These labels were given to me because of my love for missions and others. "The girl who smiles," "the girl who loves," "Christlike," "the girl who loves giving more than taking," and "the teddy-bear girl"—I got these as I grew in Christ. I will always be growing, and I know I am not perfect. Labels are removable for a reason. It is so God can make us new ones for His glory.

> This means that anyone who belongs to Christ has become a new person. The old life is gone; a new life has begun! (2 Corinthians 5:17)

The Longest Wait

June 23, 2015

All your life, you hear the words "Follow your dreams" and "You can be anything you want to be." My dreams changed as I got older. Not just because I got older, but because I also became a believer. I never thought I would be doing mission work or wanting to be a speaker. Over time, all I wanted to do was help people, serve the best way I knew how, and share the story that God had given me. However, it seems like sometimes, God has also given me the longest wait of my life. I want to be a speaker/mission worker because I feel like that is what God has placed in my heart. There have been many times when I wanted to give up on being a speaker because of the negative feedback from others. I choose not to give up for two reasons. Number 1: If you ever meet me, I am not the type to give up on anything, and if I do, something is wrong with me. Number 2: If I give up on my dream, I have also given up on God. I cannot give up on God when He has made it possible for me to do the impossible. I do think we need to be more careful with the words "Follow your dreams" and "You can be anything you want to be" because when you just can't seem to get there yet, it can be a huge letdown. I don't just give up because someone tells me to.

You never know the deep hopes and dreams of someone's life or the desires God has placed in a person's heart. Words can crush a person's spirit if we are not careful.

> Don't use foul or abusive language. Let everything you say be good and helpful, so that your words will be an encouragement to those who hear them. (Ephesians 4:29)

For Granted

June 26, 2015

Throughout my life, I have seen so many people take things for granted, even some of the most basic things in life like walking, normal everyday needs, money, cars, and just knowing that everything is going to be taken care of. There are things that I have also taken for granted. The fact that I can carry a Bible everywhere I go without being killed is a blessing in itself, but there are things I have seen people take for granted—things that are a challenge for me every day. I once was not able to walk, and today, though it can be a struggle, I am walking. So I don't take walking for granted. I once was not able to hold forks, crayons, or pencils in my hand, so I don't take feeding myself, writing, or coloring for granted. The things you are able to do on a regular basis are things I had to work for, so don't take it for granted. I once did not know Jesus, so I don't take heaven for granted. What are you taking for granted?

My question to you is simple. What do you take for granted without even realizing it?

> Since we are receiving a Kingdom that is unshakable, let us be thankful and please God by worshiping him with holy fear and awe. (Hebrews 12:28)

> Devote yourselves to prayer with an alert mind and thankful heart. (Colossians 4:2)

Don't Give Yourself Away

June 28, 2015

For some reason, people think that the minute you enter middle school, you are automatically going to start dating. I, on the other hand, did not, one of the reasons being I was homeschooled in middle school and am an only child; so my options were very slim. I also had no interest in wanting to date, not only because I was just in middle school, but also because I had no plans of being married anytime soon. I understand middle schoolers think status is everything, but why are you dating if you are not even old enough to be married? You can't honestly say you are ready to truly love someone because odds are, you don't know what love is. People today still ask me if I'm dating, and my answer is no. Why? Because I know what love is, I know what I'm looking for in a husband, and I'm willing to wait. Whoever I marry must love God first because if not, then he cannot love me. I only want to be married one time and to one person. Why would I want to get married and give my heart away and then get a divorce and give my heart away to someone else? If I do that, then that person will not have my whole heart, and that person will be missing a part of me. Whoever I date will not have all of me, but who I marry will. And the only reason we would get married is because we could better serve God together than we could apart. Girls, please be careful and don't give yourself away!

Dear middle schooler, high schooler, and college student, I wrote this blog with you in mind. I care too much about you not to tell you these things.

> Don't be concerned about the outward beauty of fancy hairstyles, expensive jewelry, or beautiful clothes. (1 Peter 3:3–4)

One Nation under God

July 5, 2015

> I pledge allegiance to the flag of the United States of America, and to the Republic for which it stands, one Nation under *God*, indivisible, with liberty and justice for all. (emphasis added)

What happened to "one nation under *God*"? People wonder why there are so many issues going on in the world and why children and teens are having so many problems in school. We have taken *God* out of school and slowly began to take *God* out of our daily life almost like He is nothing. People ask me all the time how I have the strength to make it through every day. It is because I have not taken *God* out of my life. If you want to see more love in your school, at work, and in the world, then be *love* because *God* is *love*. Stop complaining and take action because our military doesn't just fight for nothing. They fight for us, and they love this country. God made you for a purpose. He may have made you to fix or make a change in a problem in the world. Go find it! Don't wait for someone else to do it for you!

> Then if my people who are called by my name will humble themselves and pray and seek my face and turn from their wicked ways, I will hear from heaven and will forgive their sins and restore their land. (2 Chronicles 7:4)

The "Jesus Brand"

July 7, 2015

I think buying top name-brand clothes is crazy. Why would you pay fifty dollars for one shirt when you can go to another store and find the same shirt for way cheaper? I remember being looked down on so many times just because I did not have name-brand clothes. The few times kids asked me what I was wearing, when I told them, they would walk away or ask me why I did not have name-brand clothes. Truth be told, I don't care what I'm wearing as long as it fits, they match, and I look cute in it. Why does it matter what name is on it? The only name I want to wear is the "Jesus brand," and that does not mean clothes have to be boring. It means I am comfy in my own skin and can feel good at the same time. Wearing the Jesus brand is so much easier because you don't worry about what everyone is wearing, and you can honor God at the same time. What are you wearing?

The clothes you wear say something about you even if you don't realize it. I'm not saying this to make you feel bad at all. Don't misunderstand me when you read this either. I like to dress up, be casual, or have a pajama day when it's raining and cold. I wear bathing suits and everything in between. But I also have some class and enough respect for myself and for others not to show you everything because I know who I represent. I can do all of this without breaking the bank.

My question for you is not only "What are you wearing?" but "What do your clothes say about you, and how do you carry yourself?"

That is why I tell you not to worry about everyday life—whether you have enough food and drink, or enough clothes to wear. Isn't life more than food, and your body more than clothing? Look at the birds. They don't plant or harvest or store food in barns, for your heavenly Father feeds them. And aren't you far more valuable to him than they are? Can all your worries add a single moment to your life? (Matthew 6:25–27)

Heroes

July 10, 2015

All too often, we think heroes always have to have a cape and mask and save the world. What about bravery, honesty, strength, courage, and integrity? The truth is, sometimes there are many heroes that never get any credit for what they do. Missionaries and teachers are some of the hardest-working people, and they never seem to be called heroes. Why not? Missionaries give up almost everything they have and never ask for anything. They also will work and serve for no money because they are not serving you; they are serving God. Schoolteachers work like crazy to make sure your child has the best education. They spend endless hours on lesson plans and have a major impact on a child's life, so much so to the point of influencing who they become when they're grown. I myself do mission work and never ask for anything except your support. My school teachers have become my family because I have been so privileged to have them in my life after I was done with school. They have been the ones that have had the most impact in my life, and they don't wear masks or capes. Heroes are the people who work behind the scenes and ask for nothing. I have cerebral palsy, but that is not what makes me a hero. I'm not sure what makes me a hero. What I do know is that I have the strength to live with cerebral palsy every day, and I don't wear a mask or a cape.

> But you desire honesty from the womb,
> teaching me wisdom even there. (Psalm 51:6)

To the faithful you show yourself faithful; to those with integrity you show integrity. (Psalm 18:25)

He gives power to the weak and strength to the powerless. (Isaiah 40:29)

So be strong and courageous! Do not be afraid and do not panic before them. For the Lord your God will personally go ahead of you. He will neither fail you nor abandon you. (Deuteronomy 31:6)

The Heart

July 12, 2015

What comes to your mind when you think of the heart? The heart is the most important organ in the body because it keeps the rest of the body going. It is also the most fragile. I am no longer talking about the physical heart. What about your heart? Throughout life, it gets broken, beaten, and worn down, but it can also be cheered up, warmed, and loved. A lot of emotions go into the heart, and all too often, we look past those like they are nothing. You can know somebody like the back of your hand and never truly know the heart of that person. Or as your relationship grows, you realize that your heart is broken from something in that past, and you begin to heal together. I think we are way too careless with the heart, and even though we might not mean to break it, we often do so without knowing it. Then all we do is put Band-Aids over the problem and never fix it. The heart can only take so much of being broken and beaten before it dies, and if the heart dies, then the body does too. If the heart it so fragile, then why are we so careless?

Let's be honest. Life is hard. I want to take a minute and ask you a hard question. How is your heart? Is it broken, bruised, beaten, or worn down from putting Band-Aids over big problems? Does your heart have joy, peace, and compassion? Don't dwell on it for a long time but really think about it for a minute and be honest with yourself. It's just you and God right now. He can handle it.

On a personal note, my heart is all of these, but this has allowed me to be very sensitive to others and have a lot of compassion. Now take a minute and answer the hard question.

How is your heart?

> And I will give you a new heart, and I will put a new spirit in you. I will take out your stony, stubborn heart and give you a tender, responsive heart. (Ezekiel 36:26)

> The sacrifice you desire is a broken spirit. You will not reject a broken and repentant heart, O God. (Psalm 51:17)

> A glad heart makes a happy face; a broken heart crushes the spirit. (Proverbs 15:13)

Who Is Richer?

July 15, 2015

I am not rich, according to the world. I still live at home, I made minimum wage at my first job. I made just above minimum wage at my second job. I am nineteen, and according to the world, I can't make much of a difference. What little money I had, I would tithe, and I would save whatever I could. But all too often, I found myself taking the money I had saved to help someone else, or I would save money for a mission trip. My mom would get so aggravated with me because I hardly ever buy anything for myself. One of the greatest joys I have found is to see someone else smile even if it meant giving all the money I had. One of my favorite things you could ever give back to me are hugs, and those come for free. I would rather do something to glorify God and make someone smile than have a big fancy house and be a millionaire, because, in the end, I can't take any of that to heaven. I would rather store my belongings in heaven than on earth because my reward in heaven will be much greater than anything you could give me on earth. I am rich because I have worked hard to get where I am today. But most importantly, I am using the talents God has given me. And I have invested in those.

So who is richer, me or you?

There is nothing wrong with having things that you enjoy, but when that becomes your only priority, it can become a problem. If you are using the things that you own to be better than someone else or to keep up with the society we live in, you will not only become hollow on the inside because you can't keep up with other people and what they may have, but you will always be in debt or broke. I want to always be able to keep a "heavenly mindset" because the things I store up in heaven will last forever.

I would rather make a difference in the world now and have my eternal reward later.

I don't have everything the world has, but I have everything I need.

> Don't store up treasures here on earth, where moths eat them and rust destroys them, and where thieves break in and steal. Store your treasures in heaven, where moths and rust cannot destroy, and thieves do not break in and steal. Wherever your treasure is, there the desires of your heart will also be. (Matthew 6: 19–21)

> Joyful is the person who finds wisdom, the one who gains understanding. For wisdom is more profitable than silver, and her wages are better than gold. Wisdom is more precious than rubies; nothing you desire can compare with her. (Proverbs 3:13-15)

> Wisdom is even better when you have money. Both are a benefit as you go through life. (Ecclesiastes 7:11)

The Most Important Choice

July 17, 2015

Sometimes I can't help but think about what the world would be like without sin. Then I think about heaven because in the beginning, we were not meant to live in sin. It's amazing to me how one choice changed the world and human nature forever. We make choices every day—whether or not to get up, what we are going to wear, what we are going to eat, what we are going to do, and where we are going to go. Our time on earth is very precious, but what do you do with the time you have? Time for us is twenty-four hours, but time to God is a flash. One choice changed the world forever, and one choice can change you forever. Do you have time to make the most important choice of your life? I don't know about you, but I want to know a life without sin, without pain, without sickness, and without death. I want heaven because when I get there, I will not have cerebral palsy anymore! For some people, the closest they are going to get to hell is earth. But for others, the closest they are going to get to heaven is earth.

Jesus paid a high price for us to pick and choose who should come.

Have you made the most important choice of your life? Have you accepted Jesus as your Lord and Savior? Have you asked Him to forgive you of all your sins and to come into your heart and life? Do you believe in Him? I want you to live forever, and I want to meet you in heaven someday. The only way to go to heaven is through Jesus Christ.

For this is how God loved the world: He gave his one and only Son, so that everyone who believes in him will not perish but have eternal life. God sent his Son into the world not to judge the world, but to save the world through him. There is no judgment against anyone who believes in him. But anyone who does not believe in him has already been judged for not believing in God's one and only Son. (John 3:16–18)

Jesus told him, "I am the way, the truth, and the life. No one can come to the Father except through me." (John 14:6)

For everyone has sinned; we all fall short of God's glorious standard. (Romans 3:23)

But God showed his great love for us by sending Christ to die for us while we were still sinners. (Romans 5:8)

For the wages of sin is death, but the free gift of God is eternal life through Christ Jesus our Lord. (Romans 6:23)

If you openly declare that Jesus is Lord and believe in your heart that God raised him from the dead, you will be saved. (Romans 10:9)

For everyone who calls on the name of the Lord will be saved. (Romans 10:13)

Water

July 19, 2015

The ocean is one of the calmest, wildest things on the planet, and yet it's just water. Water is one of the simplest things we use, but we never think about how amazing water really is. Your body needs water on a daily basis. You can live without food for a long period of time, but you cannot live without water. Everything we grow needs water, or it will die. And we also use water for our daily functions. There is one more thing we use water for, and that often gets over looked: baptism!

Baptism is an important part of our walk with Christ. Water now has a whole new meaning. Baptism means that you have accepted Christ and that you, as a new believer, want to make a public confession of Christ. It also means that you have become a new creation. You can be baptized in many different ways, but either way, they all take place in water. Water can be life changing; it is no longer just water.

Water can be beautiful if we really think about it.

After you accept Jesus as your Lord and Savior, the Bible teaches that you should be baptized. Baptism is very important in your walk with Christ. Why? Because you saying to the world that you accepted Jesus! How awesome is that? It is also confirmation for yourself that you being saved really did happen and that nothing can take your salvation. You have become a new creation in Christ!

> For we died and were buried with Christ by baptism. And just as Christ was raised from the dead by the glorious power of the Father, now we also may live new lives. (Romans 6:4)

And all who have been united with Christ in baptism have put on Christ, like putting on new clothes. (Galatians 3:27)

There is one Lord, one faith, one baptism, one God and Father of all, who is over all, in all, and living through all. (Ephesians 4:5–6)

Value of Life

July 22, 2015

When I was in school, I remember watching the other kids and wondering if they were all as good as they said they were or if they were just smiling on the outside. It breaks my heart to see the suicide rates go up, especially those of kids, teens, and young adults. What scares me even more is that I'm in that age group, and even though my life has been rough and I caught myself wondering why I am here and with cerebral palsy, I never let myself go that far. You may be wondering why this topic is very dear to my heart. It's because I have been through suicide in my own family, and the person was only sixteen years old. I was only fourteen at the time this took place. Today, I am still not the same person I was, and I never will be. The value of life has a whole new meaning, and I'm never too caught up in my own life to not care about someone else's. I have always cared about other people, but I didn't always understand the value of the time I had with them. Living with this loss is like an amputation. You learn to live without it, but you will never be the same. Don't ever be too busy to care or spend time with people because you never know when the last time you're going to see them will be. You can stop suicide. You just have to get out of your life and look into someone else's.

This is a very hard topic for me. The value of someone's life and the thought of someone taking their own life is something not everyone is going to talk about. Having this experience has made me very fragile in some areas of my life. Is there an advantage to feeling this way? Yes, because it has made me extremely observant of other people's behavior. It has made me realize that it's okay to take time out just to be with others and spend time with them. Having this experience has also made my heart soft and more compassionate than most people.

If you're reading this, we most likely may have never met. If you have ever felt like you are worthless, valueless, and that you have no purpose, my heart goes out to you right now. I want you to know that God made you, and I know for a fact that He does not make junk! That means you have a purpose; God placed you here on purpose! I may have never met you, but I love you enough to tell you that from the deepest part of my heart. I know what it's like to barely hang on, and I want you to know that you're not alone in it.

If you're reading this and you, too, have experienced suicide in your family, I want you to know that I am crying with you and for you. I wish I could say that the pain goes away, but I know it won't. You have questions that you will never know the answers to, and you will be angry at times. You can heal from it, but you will always have a scar. Take the pain and learn to love people deeply, see people deeply, and appreciate every single moment.

> You watched me as I was being formed in utter seclusion, as I was woven together in the dark of the womb. You saw me before I was born. Every day of my life was recorded in your book. Every moment was laid out before a single day had passed. How precious are your thoughts about me, O God. They cannot be numbered. (Psalm 139:15–17)

> How do you know what your life will be like tomorrow? Your life is like the morning fog it's here a little while, then it's gone. (James 4:14)

If God Can

July 25, 2015

I think it is our human nature to worry. I, for one, am the world's worst worrier. One of the things I think about the most is the future. To be honest, I did not worry so much about it until other people started to disapprove of what I wanted to do with my life. It started to feel like all anybody cared about was how much money I was going to make. It no longer mattered if I was actually happy doing something I loved to do. I love being a missionary and taking care of children, and my dream is to be a speaker. I started working on my speaking only three years ago. For some reason, people think that I am going to have my whole life planned out at nineteen. I know that my goals in life are anything but normal, but in case you haven't noticed, nothing in my life has ever been normal. So why should I start now?

Becoming a speaker doesn't just happen. It takes time and dedication. Just because I choose not to go to college does not mean I am doing nothing. College is not for everyone! If God can create the world with words; create a human being, knowing everything about them before they are even born; provide when I did not have job; take a girl with cerebral palsy and help her defeat the odds; and give me the best people I could ever want, then who am to worry? God does not make you worry. You and other people do. If I have enough faith to be a speaker and share my story with the world, then why can't I have enough faith about my future? If God has pulled you this far in life, He will pull you through the rest!

We may have the right motives, our hearts may be right, and we may care about what someone does with their life. There is nothing wrong with that, but be careful! God calls different people to do different things. It is not our job to determine what that may be.

Are you a worrier? If so, what do you worry about, and how does worrying make the situation better?

I fight this! People have adopted worry, stress, and anxiety as a normal part of life, but we have it wrong! God does not call us to live this way! God tells us to put all our cares on Him, to not worry about tomorrow, and to trust Him completely. I know this is easier said than done. You may feel all of these things in your life, but it's our choice to stay and live in this state of mind.

Having faith in God is not only believing that God can do something. It is also believing that God will do something and that He has already done it.

> So don't worry about tomorrow, for tomorrow will bring its own worries. Today's trouble is enough for today. (Matthew 6:34)

> Give all your worries and cares to God, for he cares about you. (1 Peter 5:7)

> Don't worry about anything; instead, pray about everything. Tell God what you need, and thank him for all he has done. (Philippians 4:6)

> It is useless for you to work so hard from early morning until late at night, anxiously working for food to eat; for God gives rest to his loved ones. (Psalm 127:2)

Smile

July 25, 2015

When I was twelve years old, I found a church home that, to this day, continues to change my life. When I first got there, no one really knew who I was; they just knew that I smiled a lot. I was "the girl who smiles" until people learned my name. I have been able to work with children since I was about nine years old, and before they even knew me, they were already smiling. I was the same way when I taught karate, K3, and K4. Now I teach two-year-olds, and on my first day, all I did was smile and give them each a hug. By the end of the day, I had the whole class in my lap, reading a book, and it was only day 1.

I went to Thailand, and it was like I had been there my whole life. And it was all because of a smile. A smile can speak all languages. It doesn't matter what age you are or where you're from. A smile is also contagious. If you smile for one reason, someone else might just smile too. So turn your frown upside down so someone else's smile can be turned upside down!

Your face says everything! You don't have to speak to say anything. Your face can say it all. Your expression matters to people. What does your face say about you?

> Those who look to him for help will be radiant with joy; no shadow of shame will darken their faces. (Psalm 34:5)

School Teachers

July 30, 2015

Well, another school year is about to begin! Even though I am out of school, I can't help but think about all the kids and school teachers. It makes me think about all the school teachers that I had throughout the years and how much of an impact they all had on my life. What really gets to me is that I have been able to keep in contact with almost all of them, and today, they are like family. These are the people who saw me at my worst—surgery after surgery, braces on my legs, and how hard I worked to pass everything. My teachers knew how hard I worked, not only in my classes but also in life. One of the things that means so much to me is that they remember me after so many years and have been able to watch me grow into who I am today. School teachers have one of the most important jobs in the world, and I wish them nothing but the best for this coming school year. You never know when you might have another Rebecca in your class. Have an *awesome* school year!

I wrote this blog at the beginning of the 2015–2016 school year. I wrote this blog with the intention of touching a teacher's heart. If you are a school teacher in any way, shape, fashion, or form, I want you to know that you are not overlooked. For years, I have watched teachers be overworked, stressed, and discouraged because of the standards they have to meet, and none of them are ever paid enough. I am a speaker and a published author, but I am also a substitute teacher. That means I see this firsthand and have even experienced all of these things myself. Why did I become a substitute teacher? One of my own teachers inspired me to become one! That's how much a school teacher can influence someone. I also really love kids because deep down inside, I am one. If you're a teacher and you're reading this, I want you to be encouraged and uplifted. You are so important not only to the world but to me. You change lives, and I need you to see that!

I see you and I hear every day! Love the kids you have in your classroom. You never know what they may come from when you're not with them!

> And you yourself must be an example to them by doing good works of every kind. Let everything you do reflect the integrity and seriousness of your teaching. Teach the truth so that your teaching can't be criticized. Then those who oppose us will be ashamed and have nothing bad to say about us. (Titus 2:7–8)

> If your gift is serving others, serve them well. If you are a teacher, teach well. If your gift is to encourage others, be encouraging. If it is giving, give generously. If God has given you leadership ability, take the responsibility seriously. And if you have a gift for showing kindness to others, do it gladly. (Romans 12:7–8)

With What You've Got

August 2, 2015

We all get discouraged. We look at the problems in our life and feel overwhelmed, and if we look at the problems of the world, we feel even worse. We often feel like the problems get bigger and bigger, then we get so overwhelmed that we do nothing. Sometimes in life, we have to go with what we've got. In other words, do what you can because doing what you can is better than doing nothing at all. Then if we slowly start to do what we can, the problem will start to get smaller. For example, you cannot stop world hunger overnight, but if you start collecting one can of food a day, then you are making a difference. If you get another person to collect one can of food a day, then you are making a bigger difference. To you, it may not seem like a lot, but you still have one less person going hungry. That means the problem is slowly going away, and you did what you could. A lot of times, people would rather have you do what you can to help them instead of watching them suffer. If we look at the problems in our life the same way, maybe they would not seem so big. We also have to realize that doing something is better than doing nothing.

Discouragement is real. Your problems are real. If we look at our problems head-on and look too closely, it can cause even bigger things. What are these bigger things? I am talking about things like depression, panic attacks, insomnia, anxiety, etc. If we look at our problems for too long and constantly dwell on them, the problem will always feel overwhelming. That is way we have to look at what we've got and take it one piece at a time. Having cerebral palsy has taught me how to do this, so in some ways, I actually may be at an advantage because of the way my body works and the way my brain processes things. I really don't have any choice but to live this way. Over time, I have been taught to live this way just so my body can function in the best way possible. It takes discipline and years to learn this! My body and mind do not work like yours, but that is not always a bad thing. No matter what your problems are in life, you have to remember that God ultimately is in control of your situation and that it is not humanly possible to figure out every problem in your life in one night. Take one step at a time, and eventually, things will be resolved because taking one step and going somewhere is better than taking no steps and not going anywhere.

> Don't be afraid, for I am with you. Don't be discouraged, for I am your God. I will strengthen you and help you. I will hold you up with my victorious right hand. (Isaiah 41:10)

Worship

August 4, 2015

Music is one of my favorite things in life. Two of my favorite kinds of music are contemporary Christian and worship, and I have to admit I do like some secular music. One thing that is amazing about music is that no matter what kind it is, it can unite everybody around the world in less than a day. One artist can have a hit song, and it will spread all over the world. Worship is the same way. Music can connect us with God like nothing else, and it is an amazing feeling. You can almost be completely united with God in less than a minute, and you'll quickly realize that everybody in the room with you, no matter what the size, is united with you. You'll realize that we are all brothers and sisters in Christ and that we are all worshiping the same person, and it no longer feels like you're surrounded by a bunch of strangers. Music is my everyday escape because it reminds me of why God put me here on this earth, and it helps me get through the day and on to the next. Even on my roughest days, I still find myself lost in worship and just turn up the radio. We are all united, so why not worship the Father who made you?

Worship is different for everyone. Everyone worships differently, and depending on the atmosphere of the room, your usual style of worship may change in a minute. One thing that I think hinders us from time to time is that we care too much about what people think about us while they are standing around us, or we think about who is watching us. I have found myself feeling this way because I still have a little shyness in me. This has been a stumbling block for me at times.

Truth be told, if we are really focused on who we are singing to and who we are truly worshiping, the people around us and what they think will not matter to us. Our minds and hearts should be so focused on God that we don't even think about who is around us.

Have you ever felt like me? Have you found yourself being a shy worshiper?

> For God is Spirit, so those who worship him must worship him in spirit and in truth. (John 4:24)

> Great is the LORD! He is most worthy of praise! He is to be feared above all gods. (Psalm 96:4)

The Never-Ending Battle

August 11, 2015

I am a Christian. That means I'm in a battle every day of my life, not only with cerebral palsy but also with Christ and the devil. We have a choice to make every day to choose to live like the world or like Christ. When I was in tenth grade, I had one of the biggest battles of my life. I questioned my own salvation to the point of barely living for the next three years. I was in tears almost constantly, and I could not sleep or make it to the next school day without talking to my teacher about what was going on. This took over my every thought. I lived in fear of the thought that I was not saved. Nobody would ever expect me to think this way, but even the strongest Christians have the never-ending battle of good and evil. Today, I no longer question my salvation, and I know that I am saved. But the battle between the world and Jesus will not end until the day I'm in heaven. I know the battle is never-ending. But today I have the strength to face evil and to choose good like never before. I also know that my home in heaven is paid for in full and that Jesus paid for it all.

Doubt and fear are one of the strongest tools the enemy likes to use against us. The enemy knows our weaknesses. He knows how to trigger everyone in his own way to make us break down. It's our job to be able to recognize the lies he tells us and to see the ways it can affect how we live. When I was going through this time in my life, it was agonizing! I was at one of the weakest times of my life. What I did not understand was that not only was I eternally saved from the moment I accepted Jesus, but I also was not strong enough to recognize what was really happening to me. I let doubt and fear cripple me to the point of being mentally and emotionally exhausted. I was uncertain about myself and completely lost my focus. That is exactly what the enemy wants! He wants you in so much distress that you can't recognize him! If you're not in a battle right now, you will be in one soon. If you're in a battle now, surrender, and He will bring you out in due time.

> When doubts filled my mind, your comfort
> gave me renewed hope and cheer. (Psalm 94:19)

> Stay alert! Watch out for your great, the devil. He prowls around like a roaring lion, looking for someone to devour. (1 Peter 5:8)

You're the Lighthouse

August 12, 2015

One of my favorite places to go is the beach because it is one of the most relaxing places to go. Most people like going in the daytime, but I like going at night because I love to see all the lights from the city and look for sand crabs. The best part about the lights at night is the lighthouse. The lighthouse is amazing not only because of how it looks but because of what it does. The lighthouse helps guide ships back to land in case they are lost. This is a sign of hope. The lighthouse is the only thing shining in the complete darkness of the ocean. You could be a lighthouse! You don't know whose life you could be a lighthouse in. You could be one of the most amazing things in someone's life. You could be the light shining in complete darkness. You could be the hope leading someone back home. You are a lighthouse, encouraging and giving someone hope!

Have you ever thought of yourself as a lighthouse? We never really know the full impact we may have in somebody's life. I have had many lighthouses in my life. I would not be who am today if it were not for some of the lighthouses in my life. Wandering around and feeling like you're lost at sea in the dark is a horrible feeling, and you shrink in size on the inside. You feel abandoned and alone, like nobody sees you. I've been there many times. I have needed a lighthouse before to help me find my way, but I have also been a lighthouse for someone else. One thing I found out is that it is okay to still find a way to be a lighthouse while your lighthouse is being repaired. If you take an interest in someone else's life, it shines the light on them and gets your mind off yourself.

> Then Jesus asked them, "Would anyone light a lamp and then put it under a basket or under a bed? Of course not! A lamp is placed on a stand, where its light will shine." (Mark 4:21)

> Jesus spoke to the people once more and said, "I am the light of the world. If you follow me, you won't have to walk in darkness, because you will have the light that leads to life." (John 8:12)

The Rainbow

August 15, 2015

Have you ever thought about the stories of the Bible? They all have different lessons to be learned, and they teach us how to love, trust, and be like Jesus. They are living, breathing examples of God's work, and even though people think they're ancient and don't apply in today's world, they apply now more than they ever have. No matter how old the Bible is, we still live with the same sinful nature that we always have, which means the Bible still applies.

One of the stories I think about is the story of Noah. This story shows Noah's willingness to trust and obey God. It also shows that God keeps His promises—not some but all promises, which also proves God's faithfulness. In the story of Noah, it rained for forty days and forty nights. Noah built a boat to save his family and the animals. Then God flooded the earth because of all the sin in the world. God got fed up with His own creation, so He destroyed it. At the end, God sent the rainbow as a promise that He would never flood the earth again.

The rainbow is beautiful because it is a sign that God keeps His promises and that He is still present in our world today. The world today has taken God's beautiful sign of faithfulness and turned it into a sign of the enemy. I might be crazy, but I have no doubt that God will show up. And it will be in a way we have never seen before. It breaks my heart to know we have come this far.

> I have placed my rainbow in the clouds. It
> is the sign of my covenant with you and with all
> the earth. (Genesis 9:13)

When I see the rainbow in the clouds, I will remember the eternal covenant between God and every living creature on earth." (Genesis 9:16)

Who Are You?

August 17, 2015

As individuals, we wear many hats. I'm Rebecca, but what does that mean? How many hats do I wear? Am I the same person everywhere I go, or do I change depending on where I am? What about you? Are you the same person everywhere you go, or do you change? This can be a dangerous question because we can change in a minute. We can be one way at work and another way at home or at church. You can have a bad day at work then come home and let whatever happened at work impact everybody in the house. You can go to church and be on your best behavior and be a completely different person at home because no one knows what happens behind closed doors. There is so much in our life that we can hide because we think that if we expose something in our life, it automatically makes us a bad person. That is not true. If you expose something in your life, it can bring relief and healing. It will also put other people to the test to see if they love you for who you are or if they love you for who they thought you were. So I only have one question.

Who are you?

People and their personalities are fascinating to me. The true test here is this: Can you be honest with yourself? Do you change based on your surroundings, friends, atmosphere, or even when you're at home? If so, is it in a good or bad way? And why? Are you willing to bring even the hardest things into the light to make it better?

Jesus Christ is the same yesterday, today,
and forever. (Hebrews 13:8)

A Spiritual Birthday

August 21, 2015

Birthdays are one of the coolest things to me. I love being able to celebrate a birthday with someone I love and care about because if they were never born, I would not have the wonderful opportunity to be a part of their life. I also like giving away gifts and eating birthday cake. Spiritual birth is the same way but better. Being born again in Christ is the best birthday you could ever have because you have received the best gift of all time—eternal life. You also have many gifts that follow: love, joy, peace, patience, kindness, goodness, faithfulness, gentleness, and self-control. Those are the fruits of the spirit, which you should begin to show because Christ lives in you. You also begin to find out what spiritual gifts you have. Those are given to you by the Holy Spirit, but it is up to you to find out what they are. The best part about having a "spiritual birthday" is that you now have the greatest guest of all time in your life—Jesus Christ, and He has brought you more gifts than you could ever dream of. Jesus loves to celebrate birthdays because He loves and cares about you, and He is the one who created your birthday!

Being born again means you have accepted Christ and that you have been baptized. It also means there's something extra special living inside you. The Holy Spirit lives inside you! The Holy Spirit's job is to help you be more like Christ. He's your helper, guide, friend, and convictor so that you can start to show the fruits of the Spirit.

> Jesus replied, "I tell you the truth, unless
> you are born again, you cannot see the Kingdom
> of God." (John 3:3)

For you have been born again, but not to a life that will quickly end. Your new life will last forever because it comes from the eternal, living word of God. (1 Peter 1:23)

But the Holy Spirit produces this kind of fruit in our lives: love, joy, peace, patience, kindness, goodness, faithfulness, gentleness, and self-control. There is no law against these things! (Galatians 5:22–23)

But when the Father sends the Advocate as my representative that is, the Holy Spirit he will teach you everything and will remind you of everything I have told you. (John 14:26)

Show the Love

August 24, 2015

There are three words we all like to hear: I love you. Those three words get used a lot, but there is a difference between hearing those words and actually showing them or actually meaning what you say. In some cases, I think we use these three words carelessly and say it back just because we feel obligated to. Other times, we may not say it enough to someone we really do love. Saying it and meaning it is very important. But I also think showing it is even more important because actions speak louder than words. For me, I would much rather have your time, support, and hugs than anything else. I am just as human as anybody else, and as much as I love God, there are those times in life where I just want love with skin on it and be able to see your face. I say "I love you," but you know I mean it when I say it and am not afraid to show it either. Showing your love to someone may even mean coming out of your comfort zone, but I would rather you come out of your comfort zone than never experience what it truly means to love someone.

Everyone needs to hear the words "I love you" from someone who really means it. But we often forget that *love* is a verb. That means it takes action and that we need to show that person how much we love them. Your actions speak louder than your words.

If you take the time to show someone how much you love them, it shows you practice what you preach.

> "Teacher, which is the most important commandment in the law of Moses?"

Jesus replied, "'You must love the Lord your God with all your heart, all your soul, and all your mind.' This is the first and greatest commandment. A second is equally important: 'Love your neighbor as yourself.' The entire law and all the demands of the prophets are based on these two commandments." (Matthew 22:36–40)

Who Is Your Goalie?

August 26, 2015

When I was younger, I played soccer. I was the goalie. I was the one who had to block the ball from going into the goal. Most of the time, I never let the ball in the goal, but I also had times I would miss the ball and the other team would score the point. The same goes with things that come into our lives. We might block most, some, or none of the bad things in life. Then we might block out the good things in life. We may block out most, some, or none of the good things in life. It really depends on who your goalie is—God or the devil. The devil will try to block anything good from God, but God helps us block anything bad from the devil. There are those times where we miss and the other will score a point. If your goalie is God, then how many things of the world do we let into our lives? It could be music we listen to, TV shows we watch, and what we look at on the computer. Almost anything can turn bad if we let it. If your goalie is the devil, then how much more does God have to do to get your attention? How many things do we let into our lives that should not be there even if God is your goalie? Which team has more points? The hardest question is, "Who is your goalie?"

We are the gatekeepers of our minds, hearts, and bodies. Believe it or not, we have control over what we let into those three things. It is very important that we are aware of what we are putting in and out of ourselves. Why?

I like to make things simple, so I'll say it this way. If you put garbage in, you're going to get garbage to come out. If you put good in, you're going to get good to come out.

> Run from anything that stimulates youthful lusts. Instead, pursue righteous living, faithfulness, love, and peace. Enjoy the companionship of those who call on the Lord with pure hearts. (2 Timothy 2:22)

> And now, dear brothers and sisters, one final thing. Fix your thoughts on what is true, and honorable, and right, and pure, and lovely, and admirable. Think about things that are excellent and worthy of praise. (Philippians 4:8)

My Superpower

August 28, 2015

My favorite superhero is Batman. To be honest, I'm not sure why, other than I think he looks cool and I wish I had a car like his. Almost half of everything I own has the Batman logo on it, and with me being a girl, you would not think that I would like Batman so much.

All superheroes have superpowers. Having cerebral palsy, you have to learn how to have a sense of humor because it is going to be a really long hard road without it. I always thought it would really be cool to have a superpower even though I knew they were not real. Then I got to thinking and thought…cerebral palsy is my superpower! I have used my superpower (cerebral palsy) more than anything else in my life. I have to live with it every day. I really don't have a choice. But I have been able use it for God's kingdom. It also makes me different from anyone else, as if I was not different enough already. It also gives me the ability to love and care for others like no one else. There are days I still don't like having my superpower because it affects almost every part of my body. But I would not be me without it. Cerebral palsy is my superpower! What is yours?

I'm not going to lie. In my particular situation, cerebral palsy has brought me blessings, pain, and heartache all at the same time. I still get frustrated at times, but I also have found myself being grateful for it as well. It has allowed me go to places I would've never gone to if I were "normal." It has allowed me to have a massive amount of influence on people's lives because of the way I live my life. I am always grateful to be who I am instead of who I could be. It has caused me to be sensitive to people and their specific needs.

It has also taught me about wisdom, patience with others and myself, how to love, and how to be creative. Most importantly, it has allowed me to be used by God in ways that would never have happened without cerebral palsy.

Half of the battles we face in life are about your perspective—on how you're able to see them.

I am able to see cerebral palsy as a super power.

> Wisdom is a tree of life to those who embrace her; happy are those who hold her tightly. (Proverbs 3:18)

> A glad heart makes a happy face; a broken heart crushes the spirit. (Proverbs 15:13)

This Little Light of Mine

August 31, 2015

> This little light of mine, I'm gonna let
> it shine! Let it shine! Let it shine! Let it shine!
> (Odetta, "This Little Light of Mine")

I remember singing this song when I was little, fully knowing what it means, but what I did not know was how hard it actually could be. In today's world, it seems to get harder and harder, and whatever light you have starts out bright then gets dimmer and dimmer before it goes out. The Bible said to consider it a blessing to be persecuted for your faith. That does not always mean being killed for your faith. It could mean a number of things like doing the right thing when no one is watching you or truly standing alone for what is right when everyone else turns the other way. Standing alone takes courage, but courage stands strong. There are many times throughout my own life where I have stood alone, but I have seen the blessing of standing alone. My light may grow dim, but I never want to get to a place where it completely goes out. This little light of mine, I will *always* let it shine! Let it shine! Let it shine! Let is shine!

Is your light still shining, or has it grown dim over time?

> You are the salt of the earth. But what good
> is salt if it has lost its flavor? Can you make it
> salty again? It will be thrown out and trampled
> underfoot as worthless.
> You are the light of the world—like a city
> on a hilltop that cannot be hidden. No one lights

a lamp and then puts it under a basket. Instead, a lamp is placed on a stand, where it gives light to everyone in the house. In the same way, let your good deeds shine out for all to see, so that everyone will praise your heavenly Father. (Matthew 5:13–16)

Jesus Loves Me

September 3, 2015

We sang this song over and over as kids. We learned it when we were little, and we believed every word and knew that it was true without giving it a second thought. As we get older, that childlike faith goes away, and it is hard to believe that Jesus still loves us, especially after we realize how much sin is in our life. I am still very young, but I have faith in God. I know that Jesus loves me, but there have been times that it was hard to believe Jesus loves me no matter what. I can't help but try to have that childlike faith because without it, I would not be able to do any of the things I'm able to do today, and I do some really crazy stuff! It is still hard for me to comprehend how much Jesus loves me. I don't think any of us will fully grasp how much Jesus loves us. What I do know is that Jesus gave His life on the cross for us and that is the ultimate sacrifice.

> Jesus loves me, this I know, for the Bible tells me so. Little ones to him belong; they are weak, but he is strong. Yes, Jesus loves me! Yes, Jesus loves me! For the Bible tells me so! (Anna Bartlett Warner, "Jesus Loves Me")

This is one of my favorite songs, and it has always been close to my heart. I think it's special to me because my dad was not always the safest person to be with, and my parents are divorced. I did not always have a safe environment. When I would go to bed at night, I would lay in the dark and try to go to sleep. I would always sing this song quietly to myself, and I would eventually fall asleep. The song "Jesus Loves Me" has always given me a sense of security, and when

I did not feel love, the song reminded me that I was so very loved by Jesus.

My hope for you when you read this today is that you are reminded of how much you are loved and that you always will be loved by the Savior, Jesus Christ.

> How precious is your unfailing love, O God! All humanity finds shelter in the shadow of your wings. (Psalm 36:7)

> Even if my father and mother abandon me, the Lord will hold me close. (Psalm 27:10)

People Like Me

September 9, 2015

If you're anything like me, you are the type of person who makes sure everybody else has what they need before you take care of your own needs. You are also the kind of person to encourage others no matter what you may be going through, and even if you're the one needing encouragement. Even though these are both good traits to have, I found that sometimes they get me into trouble. I have gotten so used to encouraging others and making sure everybody else has what they need that I have almost become numb to my own feelings and needs. I am encouraging people so much that they have called me the motivator. That is a great name to have, but there comes a time where the motivator needs encouragement. Encouragement is very important because it is something that everybody needs, even the people like me.

Ever since I was really little (I mean as early as preschool age), I have always had a sincere heart and genuine concern for others. I can even remember getting awards for it in school. I am a "people watcher"; I notice everything! One of my teachers even called me her most concerned student. As I have gotten older, this part of me has become very solid. When I went into ministry, I gave everything I had. Now people remind me and teach me about self-care because I forget about taking care of myself. I say all of this to mean, even the most loving, happiest, most encouraging, and most giving people like me need everything you need.

For God chose to save us through our Lord
Jesus Christ, not to pour out his anger on us.

Christ died for us so that, whether we are dead or alive when he returns, we can live with him forever. So encourage each other and build each other up, just as you are already doing. Dear brothers and sisters, honor those who are your leaders in the Lord's work. They work hard among you and give you spiritual guidance. Show them great respect and wholehearted love because of their work. And live peacefully with each other.

Brothers and sisters, we urge you to warn those who are lazy. Encourage those who are timid. Take tender care of those who are weak. Be patient with everyone.

See that no one pays back evil for evil, but always try to do good to each other and to all people.

Always be joyful. Never stop praying. Be thankful in all circumstances, for this is God's will for you who belong to Christ Jesus. (1 Thessalonians 5:9–16)

Thank God

September 11, 2015

For me, tithing is very important. It is my one opportunity to bless God with what He has provided me with. It is so much more than just giving 10 percent of my income. I started tithing when I was fourteen or fifteen years old. One of the reasons I started so young is because I wanted it to become a habit for me. That way, when I got older, it would be automatic and never a question. Another reason why I started so young is because I understood what tithing was and wanted to obey God's Word. I wanted to give God what belonged to Him. When it comes down to it, all the money I make belongs to God because He is the one who provided it. I love to bless God with what He has given me, but that is not only reason why I tithe. I tithe not only because it belongs to God but because He has blessed me so much throughout my life. How could I not give back to God? I am not rich by any means, but tithing is not about being rich. Tithing is about thanking God for what you do have, not for what you don't have.

> "Bring all the tithes into the storehouse so there will be enough food in my Temple. If you do," says the Lord of Heaven's Armies, "I will open the windows of heaven for you. I will pour out a blessing so great you won't have enough room to take it in! Try it! Put me to the test!" (Malachi 3:10)

> Give, and you will receive. Your gift will return to you in full—pressed down, shaken

together to make room for more, running over, and poured into your lap. The amount you give will determine the amount you get back. (Luke 6:38)

You must set aside a tithe of your crops—one-tenth of all the crops you harvest each year.

Bring this tithe to the designated place of worship the place the Lord your God chooses for his name to be honored and eat it there in his presence. This applies to your tithes of grain, new wine, olive oil, and the firstborn males of your flocks and herds. Doing this will teach you always to fear the Lord your God. (Deuteronomy 14:22–23)

God's Story

September 14, 2015

If I tell you my story, then I want you to hear *love*. If I tell you my story, then I want you to hear the *kindness* of Jesus. If I tell you my story, then I want you to hear the *grace* of God. If I tell you my story, then I want you to hear about my *freedom* from my sin. If I tell you my story, then I want you to hear about *overcoming* the odds. If I tell you my story, then I want you to hear about *life*. If I tell you my story, then I want you to hear *him* and not me. If I tell you my story, then I want you hear *God's* story because my story is *His* story. I have told my story to one. I have told my story to hundreds. But whenever I speak, I want to speak because of *Him*.

What does your story tell about you?

> Then I heard a loud voice shouting across the heavens, "It has come at last salvation and power and the Kingdom of our God, and the authority of his Christ. For the accuser of our brothers and sisters has been thrown down to earth the one who accuses them before our God day and night. And they have defeated him by the blood of the Lamb and by their testimony." (Revelation 12:10–11)

I Am Guilty

September 18, 2015

When most people think about being guilty, they think about committing a crime or going to jail. What about being guilty as a Christian? Is Jesus so evident in your life that you could be convicted of being a Christian? As I live my life, I want people to notice something different about me other than the fact that I have cerebral palsy. If you are a Christian, you should be set apart from the world. But have I set myself apart enough to be guilty of being a Christian, or do I look like the rest of the world? If you were to put me on trial and convict me of being a Christian, what an honor it would be! That means that I would have done my job as a Christian and lived to honor Christ in every portion of my life, not just a part of it. I am proud to have Jesus in my life, and I am not afraid to proclaim it. I am guilty, and I love it! If I am going to be proclaimed guilty, this it is the one thing I want to be guilty of!

Have you ever thought about being "guilty" in this way? Is Jesus so evident in your life that you could be convicted of being a Christian?

> Don't copy the behavior and customs of this world, but let God transform you into a new person by changing the way you think. Then you will learn to know God's will for you, which is good and pleasing and perfect. (Romans 12:2)

> But as for me, I will always proclaim what God has done; I will sing praises to the God of Jacob. (Psalm 75:9)

Inside the Grave

September 20, 2015

Inside the grave, there is death. Inside the grave, there is a loss. Inside the grave, there is sadness, *but then* my savior came! Inside the grave, there is life! Inside the grave, there is a gain! Inside the grave, there are no more tears! Inside the grave, there is victory over death! Inside the grave, there is light and no darkness, and because of my Savior, this is possible. Without my Savior, there is no life, no gain, more sadness, and more pain than you could ever dream of and no victory over death. Inside the grave, there is nothing but darkness, no light. That is the difference my Savior makes! He is the difference between life and death. He is my Savior and the deep joy that dwells inside me no matter what happens. That is what my Savior does! This can only happen if He lives in you and becomes *your Savior*!

> For the Lord delights in his people; he crowns the humble with victory. (Psalm 149:4)

> But thank God! He gives us victory over sin and death through our Lord Jesus Christ. (1 Corinthians 15:57)

Running the Race

September 20, 2015

I have been told many things. I have been told that I am nothing and that I am useless. I have been told that I am worthless and that I will never become anything in life. It is so much easier to believe the lies of what people say than the truth about what God says about you. I have to admit that I have given in to these lies before, but that was before I started running the race God has for me. I am not running for people and their race. I am running God's race. The reason I want to be a speaker is because I don't want any more kids, youth, or adults hearing any more of the lies that I have heard. I also go to different parts of the world to do God's work. That is a long way from being nothing. Which do you think I want? One more person going to heaven, or a little bit more money? In the end, I can't take any of the things I have with me to heaven. The only thing I can take is my soul. I am running the race God has for me, not yours, because what God said about me is more important than what people have told me. And His words last forever.

Words are powerful, and the way we think about ourselves is powerful. It's so easy to give in to what people say about us as well as their opinions and thoughts about ourselves. I think one of the biggest challenges we face as humans is the approval of people. We are constantly battling between the approval of people and staying true to ourselves and who God made us to be, especially if we've chosen a path that clearly makes no sense to others, but you know what you've called to do. It doesn't make sense to other people, but it's clear as day to you. This could be almost anything—a lifestyle change, a new job, a new relationship (romantic or unromantic), a new house, or just simply trying to live a life that pleases God. Why do I know so much about this? Because this is a battle for me almost every day. I am careful about who I let influence my life, and I have learned how to keep running the race even when people try to make me fall. I have also learned that not everybody gets to have a say-so in my life.

It is okay for you to have boundaries on other people's opinions, thoughts, and words in your life. It is your job to become spiritually and mentally strong enough to decide who gets to have an opinion on the life you are trying to live or desire to have has a Christian.

> Therefore, since we are surrounded by such a huge crowd of witnesses to the life of faith, let us strip off every weight that slows us down, especially the sin that so easily trips us up. And let us run with endurance the race God has set before us. (Hebrews 12:1)

> I am with those who are weak, I share their weakness, for I want to bring the weak to Christ. Yes, I try to find common ground with everyone, doing everything I can to save some. I do everything to spread the Good News and share in its blessings.
> Don't you realize that in a race everyone runs, but only one person gets the prize? So run to win! All athletes are disciplined in their training. They do it to win a prize that will fade away, but we do it for an eternal prize. So I run with purpose in every step. I am not just shadowboxing. I discipline my body like an athlete, training it to do what it should. Otherwise, I fear that after preaching to others I myself might be disqualified. (1 Corinthians 9:22–27)

To Build a House

October 2, 2015

One day, I hope to have a house of my own. I want a house that is built strong and that can withstand almost anything that comes its way. I don't expect anything fancy. I want what I need without going over the top. This is how I want to build my house. I want a strong foundation and a door that is open to anyone. I want a house that gives second chances. I want a house that is built with love and not hate, and most importantly, I want a house that is built on God. He is strong and can withstand anything. He does not expect my house to be fancy and over the top. His door is open to anyone, and He gives second chances. He is love and not hate. This is how I want to build my house because if my house is built on God, then I have everything I need for my house. It is not about what is in the house. It is about who lives in your house.

What is your house built on, and who is living in it?

Anyone who listens to my teaching and follows it is wise, like a person who builds a house on solid rock. Though the rain comes in torrents and the floodwaters rise and the winds beat against that house, it won't collapse because it is built on bedrock. But anyone who hears my teaching and doesn't obey it is foolish, like a person who builds a house on sand. When the rains and floods come and the winds beat against that house, it will collapse with a mighty crash. (Matthew 7:24–27)

A house is built by wisdom and becomes strong through good sense. (Proverbs 24:3)

Christians Just Want to Have Fun

October 5, 2015

People think you can't have fun being a Christian. That is so far from being the truth. Being a Christian and having fun is the best because it is innocent fun—no drugs, no alcohol, no sex, no wrecks, and no consequences, just innocent fun. I have had a lot of fun being Christian. I played games in my youth group, gone on mission trips, gone to youth camp at the beach, had bonfires with friends, and gone on retreats. There was one time in particular, at youth group game night, where we had a race between three people to see who could eat three Snickers bars and drink a can of Mountain Dew the fastest. I did this and almost threw up…but I won! Having innocent fun is the best because there is no mess to clean up. You also don't have a hangover with the same problems you passed out with. I had a blast! Being a Christian is not boring. It's fun! Christians just want to have fun!

Dear middle schoolers and high schoolers,

I wrote about this with you in mind. Being a Christian or becoming one is not about a list of dos and don'ts. Please don't get the wrong impression and think you can never do anything or have anything because you're a Christian. I just don't want you to end up in a bad situation that you're not ready for and can't get yourself out of.

Girls, if you're in school right now and you don't have a boyfriend, it is absolutely okay that you don't have one. If you do have a boyfriend by your own choice, that's fine too. But if he is trying to get you to do things that you don't want to do and that you know is not right, then he needs to hit the highway! The right person will respect you for who you are and for standing up for what is right.

Boys, doing drugs and smoking with a group of friends is not cool. It is very unattractive, and it makes your breath smell bad. Girls don't want to smell that! Girls want someone who makes them feel secure and safe and that does not throw money away on things that were not made for your body anyway. If she tries to manipulate you in any way, shape, or form, then she needs to hit the highway too! Do not let her change you into someone you know is not right.

I want you to have fun! Please do! Go have fun. There are plenty of ways to have fun without having to go back and clean it up along with shame, guilt, and regret. I don't want that for anyone!

> For you have been called to live in free-dom, my brothers and sisters. But don't use your freedom to satisfy your sinful nature. Instead, use your freedom to serve one another in love. (Galatians 5:13)

> He is so rich in kindness and grace that he purchased our freedom with the blood of his Son and forgave our sins. (Ephesians 1:7)

My Greatest Mystery

October 8, 2015

I will never completely understand Jesus. I may know a lot about Jesus and what He did, but He will always be the greatest mystery to me. How can someone be eternal and be here on earth at the same time? How can someone be higher than the highest high but closer than I can comprehend? He came has a human with unending strength but still had a heart that was tender. He was born to die and to free the slaves. He is the beauty of amazing grace. I can feel His peace as if He was beside me. He is the greatest mystery to me. I am so undeserving of His love, but He still loves me anyway. I need Him more than He could ever need me, but He still loves me and loved me even before time began. He has such a love for me that I cannot comprehend it. To me, the greatest mystery is Jesus being in love with me. I have no choice but to trust in the fact He is also God in the flesh, and that should be enough to answer all my questions.

> But let all who take refuge in you rejoice; let them sing joyful praises forever. Spread your protection over them, that all who love your name may be filled with joy. (Psalm 5:11)

I Am a Princess

October 12, 2015

Ever since I was little, I have loved Disney movies. My favorite movie is the *Lion King* because I love the story line and the music. I have to admit that I am not a huge princess fan, but I still like the movies. When I was little, I never really caught myself saying that I wanted to be a princess. I was never really into all the makeup and the big dresses. What makes me like the princesses in those movies is not only the story but their character. They always help people. They always want to love the people they are with. They are humble and smart, and they have to know how to lead others. We should be that way if we say we follow Christ, and other people should be able to tell it by our character. I am Christ's follower, so that should mean that I am willing to help others. I should show the love of Christ to the people I am with. I should always be humble, and I don't need a PhD to lead others to Christ. Princesses don't always come in a big puffy dress and makeup. Sometimes they are wearing jeans and a T-shirt. I am a princess, but it is only because I belong to the true King!

Dear woman,

We all have a little girl living way deep inside us. This is one thing I hope I never lose. It's a part of what makes up my personality. You have hopes and dreams that I know you still want to live out. As you grow up, remember that you are the daughter of the one true King! Maintain your meekness and humble heart. Lead others without pride, and remember, you don't need a PhD to tell others about Jesus. If you need to put on a big puffy dress every now and then, do it. And remember, God thought you were beautiful before you even put it on!

No matter how old you get, you will always be *His* little girl!

> She is clothed with strength and dignity, and she laughs without fear of the future. When she speaks, her words are wise, and she gives instructions with kindness. She carefully watches everything in her household and suffers nothing from laziness. Her children stand and bless her. Her husband praises her: "There many virtuous and capable women in the world, but you surpass them all!" Charm is deceptive, and beauty does not last; but a woman who fears the Lord will be greatly praised. Reward her for all she has done. Let her deeds publicly declare her praise. (Proverbs 31:25–31)

The Streets of Heaven

October 14, 2015

I am a girl, and sometimes I like to wear jewelry. But I'm not one of those people who like to spend hundreds of thousands of dollars on something so little. There are some things that I would spend a lot of money on—for example, my wedding ring, but that is something I will wear for the rest of my life. And it also has significant meaning behind it, so I would want to spend the money on it. Something I find so funny is that we spend so much money on gold and silver here on earth and that we think it is so valuable. But have you ever stopped to think about what God uses for the streets in heaven? He uses gold! What we hold so close and valuable here on earth, God uses for pavement for us to walk on in heaven! This proves that nothing is more valuable than heaven. It also proves that gold and silver are nothing to God. This means that your life, to God, is more valuable than the silver or gold you buy to wear around your neck.

One thing I learned just by watching people is that people love stuff. There is nothing wrong with having stuff. I like having things too, but it's not my main priority. We hold things that we buy so close to ourselves that we can easily forget what's really important to us. People can have so my things that they become a slave to their own debt, work their lives away, and have very little time to spend with anyone. Everything we own is temporary. You will never see a U-Haul behind a hearse.

Your life is more precious than all the stuff you own together and more. That's why God only wants you!

> Don't store up treasures here on earth, where moths eat them and rust destroys them, and where thieves break in and steal. (Matthew 6:19)

> Just as the rich rule the poor, so the borrower is servant to the lender. (Proverbs 22:7)

The Story of a Little Girl and Her Widowed Father

October 15, 2015

There was a girl who lived in a house with her father. He was widowed. The little girl wanted to be just like her mother when she grew up. She would walk around the house, wearing all her makeup and a plastic diamond necklace just like the one her mom had, except the mother's was a real diamond necklace. Every year on her birthday, as that little girl grew up, she would ask her father if she could have the necklace. The father said no. The little girl said, "Okay," but she did not understand why he would not let her wear it.

As the years went on, the answer was always no. That little girl still had on the plastic necklace, and she held on to it almost like it was the real one. The little girl grew angry at her father and said, "Why can't I wear the necklace? I will do anything to wear the necklace!" The little girl walked away, and her father thought about what she had said.

The next day, the little girl and her father sat together. The father said, "Give me the plastic necklace." The little girl said no and walked away. The next day came, and the father said, "Give me the plastic necklace." The little girl said no and walked away.

The next few weeks went by, and the answer was still no. Finally, the father said, "Give me the necklace!" commanding her to give it to him. The little girl was crying and looked up at her father as she took off the plastic necklace and gave it to him. When the father had the old necklace in his hand, he reached back and pulled out the diamond necklace that was in his pocket the whole time. He placed it around the little girl's neck and said in a soft voice, "All you had to do was give me the plastic necklace." The little girl smiled as she hugged her father.

She looked like her mother—just like she always wanted. God wants to give us the diamond necklace, but we have to be ready to give up the plastic one.

In other words, we have to give up our old way of life and be ready for the new life God has been hiding in his pocket.

> Trust in the Lord with all your heart; do not depend on your own understanding. Seek his will in all you do, and he will show you which path to take. (Proverbs 3:5–6)

> If you try to hang on to your life, you will lose it. But if you give up your life for my sake and for the sake of the Good News, you will save it. (Mark 8:35)

He's Got the Whole World in His Hands

October 18, 2015

I love it when the weather starts to change! My favorite time of the year is any time when the weather is cold. It's time for bonfires, s'mores, and hot dogs over an open fire! Even though this all sounds great, let's not forget the one who is in control of it all—God! He made the whole world with His voice, and He holds the whole world in His hands. He made the sun rise, and He made the sun set. He made the whole universe that we live in and made the Earth rotate around the sun so that we could have summer, fall, winter, and spring. He also has enough control over the Earth to make sure we don't spin off of it! If God can hold the whole world in His hands and make all of this happen, we should also know that He holds us in His hand too. God is always in control. The change in the seasons is just one of the ways He shows us!

This is just a reminder for you and for me that God is ultimately in control. He always has us in His hands even when we can't see it or have the strength to believe it.

He will never let go!

> My sheep listen to my voice; I know them,
> and they follow me. I give them eternal life, and
> they will never perish. No one can snatch them

away from me, for my Father has given them to me, and he is more powerful than anyone else. No one can snatch them from the Father's hand. (John 10:27–29)

The Lion and the Lamb

October 22, 2015

All your life, you hear about the lion and the lamb and how they represent God and Christ. This is even in the Bible. But have you ever stopped and really thought about the whole picture? The lion is the "king of the jungle," and it is one of the biggest animals created. The lamb is one of the weakest and smallest animals created. The lamb also stands for purity because it is white. God the Father is the king over all of heaven and earth just like the lion is king over all of the jungle. The son of God is the lamb of God because Christ is pure just like the lamb. The lamb was also used as a sacrifice because of its purity, just like how Christ was sacrificed for us. He was spotless and had no sin.

One thing I find interesting is that the Bible uses the lamb to represent Christ, who is strong, but the lamb is one of the weakest animals. In some cases, God will use someone we consider weak to do the things that take the most strength because the weak are the most willing to do God's work. Most people think I am weak because I have cerebral palsy. But I am strong not just because I have a black belt in karate but because I get my strength from the King of heaven and earth. Even if you are not a believer, one day, every knee will bow before the lion and the lamb.

> He gives power to the weak and strength to
> the powerless. (Isaiah 40:29)

> You must have the same attitude that Christ
> Jesus had. Though he was God, he did not think
> of equality with God as something to cling to.

Instead, he gave up his divine privileges; he took the humble position of a slave and was born as a human being. When he appeared in human form, he humbled himself in obedience to God and died a criminal's death on a cross. Therefore, God elevated him to the place of highest honor and gave him the name above all other names, that at the name of Jesus every knee should bow, in heaven and on earth and under the earth, and every tongue declare that Jesus Christ is Lord, to the glory of God the Father. (Philippians 2:5–11)

Life Does Come with a Manual

October 27, 2015

As many things as I know about life, there are some things I just don't understand. I don't understand how someone can sit back and watch human trafficking get worse every day. I don't understand how the United States can have the highest abortion rate and how someone could have no feelings whatsoever. I don't understand how someone could claim to not know right from wrong when they don't want to kill, steal, or lie because it is wrong. How do you know it's wrong? Because someone taught you it was wrong. I don't understand how someone can claim not to have morals but have some sense of boundaries. There are many things I don't understand about this world even though I know it has fallen. One thing I know is that we have had morals since the beginning of time. We just stopped acknowledging it. No matter what you try to do to take God out of the picture, He will always be in it. The Ten Commandments are the beginning of the difference of right and wrong, not to mention the fact that there are way more commandments than just the first ten. The Bible also teaches how to live a holy life that's pleasing to God. Life does come with a manual. It is called the Holy Bible.

As I watch and live in this world, I must say that at times, it makes me sad and a little angry. The world I live in today compared to the world my grandparents and even my parents grew up in sound so much better than the world I'm in today. I understand that every generation has its times of trouble and goes through things that they may not be very proud of. It just seems like today's people are angrier, sadder, greedier, more selfish, and more morally corrupt than ever. Today, we live in a world where anything goes and everything slides because we don't want anyone to be offended. There are no boundaries and no moral code, and the faith that America once had has been abandoned.

I feel like I will never get to see the "good old days," as my grandparents would say.

I have had to learn how to remain and hold on to what is good and true in a leaving culture.

> Hold on to the pattern of wholesome teaching you learned from me a pattern shaped by the faith and love that you have in Christ Jesus. (2 Timothy 1:13)

> Preach the word of God. Be prepared, whether the time is favorable or not. Patiently correct, rebuke, and encourage your people with good teaching.
> For a time is coming when people will no longer listen to sound and wholesome teaching. They will follow their own desires and will look for teachers who will tell them whatever their itching ears want to hear. (2 Timothy 4:2–3)

> Remain in me, and I will remain in you. For a branch cannot produce fruit if it is severed from the vine, and you cannot be fruitful unless you remain in me. (John 15:4)

Hope

November 1, 2015

Having cerebral palsy is not always fun, and even though I may make it look easy, it has not always been this way. It can be painful, and there have been many times where I have spent more time in a doctor's office or hospital than my own house. I have had many things done to me that you would never even think about or dream of, and I know for a fact that you would not want your own kids to go through what I have experienced. Choosing to overcome a disability is not easy. You have to have hope. When I say hope, I don't mean temporary hope. I mean real hope—the hope that one day, I will no longer have cerebral palsy and that God made me the way He wanted.

Throughout life, I have seen many things. I know the difference between real hope and temporary hope. I have seen people more disabled than me. It is because they have no hope. They have no power to overcome anything. So if I have real hope and know that I was made by God, am I disabled?

I need to ask you a question. Do you have hope? Even as Christians, we can sometimes lose hope. Christians are not exempt from feeling this way even though people may think that. Having hope is important because you are able to look forward to every day. When we lose hope, it can lead us to scary places, and it is very hard to find our way out. This is the way losing hope can cause us to become "disabled."

I want you to know that I understand what it's like to lose hope. I have fallen into this pit many times for different reasons, and I know it feels like you will never make it out. You get tired of waiting and forcing yourself to be happy. It's hard, and I know this very well. It's okay to be down for a little while, but it is not okay to stay down. Only when you do not choose to get back up and try again is when you have truly given up. Every day, when you choose to see the sun rise, it means you have not given up. There is always hope when you look at the sunshine because it is shining right back at you!

> When doubts filled my mind, your comfort
> gave me renewed hope and cheer. (Psalm 94:19)

> Rejoice in our confident hope. Be patient
> in trouble, and keep on praying. (Romans 12:12)

A Leap of Faith

November 5, 2015

I have had to make many choices in life—some good, some bad, and then there are the kind of choices you just don't want to make because you can't see the outcome. That is when you find out how much you trust God. It is the feeling of jumping off the cliff and taking a leap of faith. It is taking a leap of faith, knowing, and believing God will catch you at the bottom. Even though I can't always see the bottom, I have to know that there is something better waiting for me when I get there. It could be the dream I had been waiting on. It could be that someone needs me more than I know. It could be an amazing opportunity, or it could be God teaching me how to trust him in whole new way. We may never know until we get there. My job is to jump, learn to wait on God, and take whatever He has for me at the time.

If we are all honest, we can admit we all struggle with this from time to time. Taking a leap of faith is one of those things that is easier said than done. It doesn't matter how big or small the leap of faith is. It still matters because it's important to you.

When was the last time you had to make a decision that required you to have faith? Did you move forward, or did something stop you? If something stopped you, why did it? And did you regret it? If you moved forward, what gave you the strength to do so?

Faith shows the reality of what we hope
for; it is the evidence of things we cannot see.
(Hebrews 11:1)

Hakuna Matata

November 11, 2015

> Hakuna matata! What a wonderful phrase!
> Hakuna matata! Ain't no passing craze. It means
> no worries for the rest of your days! It's our prob-
> lem-free philosophy! Hakuna matata! (Elton
> John, "Hakuna Matata")

If only we could live life that way. I have said in the past that I am the worst worrier ever. I also said that the *Lion King* was my favorite Disney movie. I think I am always going to have that kind of nature just because I really care about people, and because it is hard not to worry about my own life. One thing I have noticed about myself is that, over time, it has gotten a little better as I learn how to put all my cares on God. Sometimes I think we have a bad habit of putting only some of our cares on God and not all of them, or we put all our cares on God and pick them back up again just after the church service is over. So did we really give them all to God? Nope! In the Bible, it said to cast all our cares on God because He is supposed to care for us. If we truly did that, I think we would all be singing "Hakuna Matata"!

Do you have the habit of giving some of your cares to God and then picking them back up again?

Maybe you have never given anything to Him and just worry and hold on to things because you don't know how not to worry.

This is a hard habit to break, but it can happen if we really want it to.

> Give all your worries and cares to God, for
> he cares about you. (1 Peter 5:7)

I Am Here to Serve

November 19, 2015

I am a Christian, but what does the word *Christian* mean? The word *Christian* means "to be Christlike." If I look back at Scripture and look at Jesus, it shows He came to give His life, but that's not all He did. Jesus came to serve, not to be served. He put on the clothes of a slave and washed His disciples' feet. He fed the hungry, healed the sick, saved a woman from being stoned, and raised people from the dead. With that being said, if I claim to be a Christian, that means everything I say and do should honor Christ. It also means that I, too, should come to serve and not be served. I know the purpose of my life is serving and giving. This is how I fulfill the purpose God has given me, and it overflows in everything I do. I am here to serve, not to be served.

Are you a Christian? If so, do you look like Jesus? If I met you, would I be able to tell you are a follower of Jesus just by the way you carry yourself in this world, or do you look and act like everyone else?

> For even the Son of Man came not to be served but to serve others and to give his life as a ransom for many. (Mark 10:45)

> But the Holy Spirit produces this kind of fruit in our lives: love, joy, peace, patience, kindness, goodness, faithfulness, gentleness, and self-control. There is no law against these things! (Galatians 5:22–23)

The Real Me

November 24, 2015

If you know me at all, you know my personality. I am very laid-back and calm, my voice is quiet, and I sound like a seven- or eight-year-old girl. I have an innocent face and would never hurt a fly. If you don't know me, this is the best way I can describe myself. I have dreams that are bigger than the world. I have a heart as big as the sea. If I know you personally, I can read you like a book. My eyes are very aware of what is happening in the world around me, and I can see straight through your heart. My ears will hear every word you tell me, and those words will always stay with me. My mouth is used to encourage, not to discourage. I use my arms to give away presents and hugs. I use my legs to walk the way Jesus walked the best way I know how. If you are close to my heart, then I hurt when you hurt. I cry when you cry. When you smile, I smile because you make me smile. I love children like they are my own. I love doing the things kids get to do because I never got to do them when I was younger. If you spend a day with me, you will realize I'm just a big kid. This is how I would describe myself. This is the real me. I hope you like me, and I hope you've gotten to know me.

I wrote this from a very personal place inside me. I did that on purpose. There is a good chance that I may never meet you in person. If I have, it was an honor to meet you. But for those of you who have not met me, I wrote this because I want you to meet me from a distance beyond this book or your computer screen. I want you to see that I am a real person. I laugh, cry, love deeply, and smile when I don't always feel like it; and I am very slow to anger. I have sick days, good days, and bad days just like you. One of the reasons I decided to take what used to be my blog and place it into this book is so you could see some of what is underneath the smile that people are used to seeing on my face.

I am personal on purpose!

> There are "friends" who destroy each other,
> but a real friend sticks closer than a brother.
> (Proverbs 18:24)

The Life of a Missionary

December 27, 2015

If you wonder what it is like being a missionary, this is the blog for you! This is the life of a missionary. You have to have unconditional love for people no matter how nice or crazy they may seem. You have to learn how to trust God more than most people. You have to be willing to put aside big fancy cars and houses and know the difference between needing and wanting. You have to take care of someone else's needs before your own. You have to know how to plan, save money, and organize projects. If you fly internationally, be prepared for airport security, jet lag, eating airplane food over and over again, bringing entertainment for layovers, and the many hours you are going to be in the air. Don't expect to sleep well when traveling by plane. You will have dry eyes so much that people will think you're on drugs. If you fly for several days in a row, be ready to not take a shower until you get to a hotel. Being a missionary is very rewarding, but it can also be very emotionally stressful. As you go to different places, you begin to see life totally differently from most people. You will begin to feel joy, love, and excitement. But even in the middle of all that, you will feel sad and heartbroken too. This is because when it is time to leave, you have already made friends and built relationships with people you never thought possible. You will be wishing they could come home with you. You will also carry God's Word everywhere you go, so be ready for life-changing moments not only in your life but in the person you are sharing the reality of eternal life with. Wherever you are, bring travel-sized Pepto because you will eat food you have never seen in your life.

Being a missionary is not easy, is it?

Next time you question me on my "easy" lifestyle, you might want to rethink it. This is the life of a missionary. Missionaries push aside the thought of living comfortably so that others can live forever.

I have to admit that I was slightly agitated when I wrote this. I love this side of my life, but there have been times where people have really frustrated me. I knew when I got called into missions that it was going to be a challenge. One thing that I was not prepared for was the constant doubting and the questioning from others. I was not ready for the mocking, laughing, and the smirks that lay across people's faces as they think being a missionary is worth nothing. The Bible does say to be ready for these things, but I was not prepared for it to come from some of the closest people in my life.

Why do I keep going through things like this?

Because Jesus did too, and so will I.

Jesus is worth it all!

> How beautiful on the mountains are the feet of the messenger who brings good news, the good news of peace and salvation, the news that the God of Israel reigns! (Isaiah 52:7)

More to Life

January 6, 2016

Sometimes I wonder how I spend my time on this earth. Do I spend it wisely? Am I living the way I say I believe? Do the words I speak match my actions? What about the people we love and care about? Do we spend enough time with them, or do we take the people in our lives for granted and expect them to always be there for another day? In my life, I have been through many losses. I lost more people while I was in high school than most people lose in their whole life. From the time I started high school and from the time I graduated, I had been through five funerals, and some of them were just months apart. The last funeral I attended was on the week of my high school graduation. Most of the people I lost were in their teens or early twenties. After going through five funerals in a row, I can't help but think the worst when someone dies. I also never know when I'm going to face another one. I have become sensitive to the deaths of others to the point of completely shutting down. Today, I try my hardest to spend time with the people I love. I don't wait until it is convenient for me. I take every chance I can. One of the things that makes me upset is when people are so consumed with their own lives and what they are doing that they don't take the time to be in someone else's life. You would be surprised what a simple phone call or even a text can mean to people. If you can't make the time to visit, then you need to take the time to call because you never know when the last phone call will be.

There is more to life than your own life!

Time is valuable, and we are not promised tomorrow. We should never assume that we or someone else has unlimited access to the next day. Make time to love, laugh, live, and hold the ones you love a little tighter. These things are good for the soul, and they can benefit you just as much as the things that keep you busy.

> How do you know what your life will be
> like tomorrow? Your life is like the morning fog
> it's here a little while, then it's gone. (James 4:14)

Be Pro-Life

January 20, 2016

My life has value and purpose. I have cerebral palsy, but does that mean my life has less value and no purpose? I came into the world two months before I was supposed to. My mom and dad had no warning of my future diagnosis, the struggles I would face, all the physical and occupational therapy, and all the surgeries I would have to go through. When parents find out ahead of time that they are going to have a baby with special needs, they are devastated and automatically think that child would have no quality of life. If you are a teenager who is pregnant and you have found out your baby will have some form of a disability, you are thinking one of three things: (1) keeping the baby, (2) adoption, or (3) abortion. If you are a teenage mother, first of all, I am very sorry that this has happened to you! Having a baby is supposed to be a joy, not a burden! I do have to say that you were either looking for love in the wrong places, or you were taken advantage of. If you are married, not married, or a teenage mother expecting a baby with a disability, I don't care what category you are in! Please don't kill your baby! Give that baby a chance to show you life! *Be pro-life!* That baby has value and a purpose for the way he/she was made! Take it from someone who knows! If I had been killed, this is what the world would have missed out on: a testimony, a missionary, a speaker, a true friend, a karate instructor, a high school graduate, a soccer player, the best babysitter ever, a dreamer, and a blogger! *You will have struggles and pain*, but this is what came after a *world changer*! That baby may not change you, but it can change someone else! *Be pro-life* because *every* child deserves a chance to change the world!

God does not make junk.
He only makes masterpieces.

> You made all the delicate, inner parts of my body and knit me together in my mother's womb. (Psalm 139:13)

Strength

January 27, 2016

What does it mean to have strength? When we think of strength, most of us automatically think about physical strength. But that is not the only kind of strength that matters. I'm not saying that it is not important to be strong, but what I am saying is that I think there are other kinds of strength that are more important. What about spiritual strength? Or having strength to overcome something you face on an everyday basis? Or having the ability to stand up for what is right when no one else will? Or doing the right thing even when no one is watching you? No one really likes to talk about that kind of strength because it will take more than just your physical strength to get through those types of things, and all of a sudden, how many pounds you can lift does not do you any good...does it?

To have spiritual strength, you have to study God's Word and face trials in life. The only way you can make it is by facing those trials with God and the people He has put in your life to hold your hand through it. I have to figure out how to face cerebral palsy, fear, divorced parents, scoliosis, and *many* other things. I know what it is like to have to overcome something every day in life, and it takes a whole lot more than just my physical strength to get through it. Having the ability to stand up for what is right is extremely important because if you don't stand up for what is right, you will fall for anything. Doing the right thing when no one is watching you means letting go of your own pride and glory. It also means you do it "just because," and you don't expect anything in return. Do something that glorifies God and not you. There is a whole lot more to strength than you think. You might be strong, but when life hits you in the face, make sure you're strong enough to pick yourself back up!

Strength should not be determined by how someone appears on the surface. It's the battles that we face in life that make us internally strong, and we have to have the desire to overcome the things we face. If you don't have that desire, your battle will overpower you.

The victory is already yours. You might just have to stretch for it to reach it.

> The Lord is my strength and my song; he
> has given me victory. (Psalm 118:14)

Inside Out

February 8, 2016

Disney came out with a movie this past year. It's called *Inside Out*. I saw this movie and thought it was great, but I could not help but think, *What if this were real?* What is going on inside your head? What would happen if we all really let the inside out? Some people hide every emotion on the inside whether it be joy, sadness, anger, fear, or disgust. If you're like me, it takes a lot for you to get angry, and sometimes you hide what you really feel. People can expect so much out of one person that it forces you to be strong all the time whether it is good or bad. You are strong for everybody else, and the one time you break down, it is almost like you're not allowed to. You hold everything in until one day, something happens to make everything come out. Then it truly is inside out. If you have joy, then you jump. If you have sadness, then you cry. If you have anger, I hope your head doesn't catch fire, but most likely, you'll say words you don't mean. If you have fear, then you hide. If you have disgust, then you don't try anything new and say, "I don't like it," before you try it. Who could forget Bing Bong! He is my favorite! I see some of myself in him. He is so outgoing and caring that he can't see what's coming, and he can't spell, just like me! The deeper question is, what would happen if we let our inside out?

Inside Out is a movie made by Disney Pixar. I highly recommend you watch this movie then come back and read this because you would be able to connect with it better. If you watch closely, there really is some truth in what I am writing about. I thought it was pretty neat that I could write a blog based on a Disney movie.

The question still remains, though.

What would happen if you let your inside thoughts or emotions come out?

> For the word of God is alive and powerful. It is sharper than the sharpest two-edged sword, cutting between soul and spirit, between joint and marrow. It exposes our innermost thoughts and desires. (Hebrews 4:12)

> You know when I sit down or stand up. You know my thoughts even when I'm far away. (Psalm 139:2)

> "My thoughts are nothing like your thoughts," says the Lord. "And my ways are far beyond anything you could imagine.
>
> For just as the heavens are higher than the earth, so my ways are higher than your ways and my thoughts higher than your thoughts. (Isaiah 55:8–9)

The Weight of the Cross

February 14, 2016

What weight in your life do you carry? We all carry weight in our lives even if we know we don't have to carry it. Sometimes we are so used to carrying the weight in our lives that we don't know what it's like to not have to carry it. What about the weight of the cross? Jesus carried the weight of the cross on His shoulders. Not only did He carry the weight of the cross, but He carried the weight of every sin, every act of terrorism, every drop of murdered blood, every broken marriage, every crime against humanity, every starving nation, every word said in hate, every theft, every lie, every moment of lust, every abandoned child, every altered lifestyle, every injustice, every grudge, every kind of bitterness, every fear, and every doubt—everyone! Jesus carried the weight of everyone. Jesus became sin for us so much that He was separated from God the Father on the night He was on the cross. He carried it so we would not have to. This is the weight of the cross. We were never meant to carry the weight of our lives on our own because Jesus already carried it for us.

What weight do you carry?

Jesus knew what He was doing when He died for us. He knew that sin, worry, and guilt would weigh us down. That's why He took it from us. Jesus was the only person that was strong enough to carry it. You were never created to carry your burdens alone.

Share each other's burdens, and in this way
obey the law of Christ. (Galatians 6:2)

Do You Believe?

February 14, 2016

I get many questions. One of the most common questions I get is "How have you been able to do so much for others?" or How do you continue to want to change the world?" The answer is simple. I believe that I can! I believe that I can change the world. I think what stops many people from helping others is that they don't believe they are changing lives or doing anything to make a difference. If you are doing something to help someone, you are making a difference, but you might not always see the difference you are making. Sometimes you just have to know you are and believe it.

I want to change the world. I want to leave a legacy when I die. I continue to change the world because one of my greatest desires in life is to help people, serve like Jesus served, and love like Jesus loved. That is part of my life as a Christian. I want to leave a mark on this world for the good. I can change the world because I believe that I can. If you don't believe you can do something before you even start, then you have already lost before you have given yourself a chance to win. I believed that I could do something, so I did! What do you believe?

Are you easily discouraged?

Do you feel as if you have lost the battle before you've even started?

I have felt these things throughout my whole life, and to be honest, if you live long enough, you will at some point.

When I was younger, I took karate and eventually became an instructor. Two of the things we learned as we were training was how to check our posture and how to check our mindset. If we did not check these things, we could lash out or become seriously injured. We had to come on the mat determined and with the mindset of believing in ourselves, giving our best effort in everything. Even if we did not win, we had to come on the mat as if we had already won. Then our physical posture would take care of itself.

I share this with you to say, "Your posture in your mind and body is everything!" If you approach something like you have already won, giving your best effort, you will win in the end. If you approach something like you have already lost before you started, you will lose.

You have to believe in yourself before anyone else will!

All you who fear the Lord, trust the Lord!
He is your helper and your shield. (Psalm 115:11)

Broken Beautifully

March 17, 2016

My view of the world is different from most, but it is only because I have been forced to look at it differently. I have viewed the world from hospital rooms, doctor's offices, school classrooms, school bus windows, wheelchairs, and airplanes. I was on the inside looking out into the world. Today, it is the complete opposite.

Now I am on the outside looking in. As I travel the world and even in my own hometown, I see broken people with broken hearts. Depression, suicide rates going up, divorce rates sky-rocketing, teen-agers with babies and eating disorders, abandoned children, and drug and alcohol abuse. That's a lot to handle for someone like me; but it should be a lot for any one. I have wondered sometimes how the world could be so broken but beautiful at the same time. The sky is blue, the sun is shining, the birds sing, the flowers grow, and the waters know exactly where to stop so we can have amazing beaches. Nothing God creates is ugly or a mistake. This includes everything in the world and every human being. Even a criminal was created by God. Everything God makes has a purpose. In other words, God does not make junk because He does not have the time to. The world is still beautiful. We are the ones who made it broken because we are broken people, but we are still beautiful because God made us. This is how I view the world—broken beautifully.

Everybody has a different opinion of the world we live in. If I were to ask you how you saw the world, what would you say?

The earth is the Lord's, and everything in it. The world and all its people belong to him. (Psalm 24:1)

The heavens are yours, and the earth is yours; everything in the world is yours you created it all. (Psalm 89:11)

His Love

April 7, 2016

One of the things that gets studied the most is the love of God. The truth is, it is indescribable, and we will never fully understand it. If someone asked me to describe it, this is the best way I could put it: His love is unchangeable. His love is what chose you. His love is louder than the lies that you hear. His love does not walk away when the world does. His love is what tells you you're not a mistake when the people in the world think you are. His love tells you that you are priceless. His love knows you inside and out.

I know the attributes of God and the characteristics of God, but those will come later. The most important thing for people to understand is the love of God because everything else after that will fall into place. There is nothing you can do to change the love that God has for you. Nothing is too big for God to handle because His love will conquer it.

It is easy to feel unloved in this life. People are people, and I think we can forget that sometimes. Words can be forgiven but not forgotten. Maybe you have never felt loved. Maybe you thought you were loved by someone, but it came out to be a lie. You might be one of those people who have never heard "I love you." You may have been taken advantage of, beaten, bruised, manipulated, and long for gentleness. Maybe the love you felt was performance-based.

I can identify with this entire paragraph.

What makes the difference?

Knowing that I can never outrun the love of God. Knowing that He loved me before I could love Him. Knowing that God's love runs deep. It's unconditional, not performance-based or manipulative. It's beautiful, and it's like no other. Nothing can take it away or separate me from it. God never leaves you or forsakes you.

He never forgets about you, and He never will!

God loves you, and He will never stop loving you!

If you encounter the love of God, you will encounter the peace of God.

> How precious is your unfailing love, O God! All humanity finds shelter in the shadow of your wings. (Psalm 36:7)

> And I am convinced that nothing can ever separate us from God's love. Neither death nor life, neither angels nor demons, neither our fears for today nor our worries about tomorrow not even the powers of hell can separate us from God's love.
>
> No power in the sky above or in the earth below indeed, nothing in all creation will ever be able to separate us from the love of God that is revealed in Christ Jesus our Lord. (Romans 8:38–39)

If I Had a Daughter

April 10, 2016

If I had a daughter, I would want her to know God made her the way that He wanted. If I had a daughter, I would want her to know that God knew her before she was even in existence. If I had a daughter, I would want her to know how special I think she is. If I had a daughter, I would want her to know that she is a gift from God because if I had her, then it would mean that I made it through a high-risk pregnancy. If I had a daughter, I would want her to know that I make mistakes and that I have never been perfect. If I had a daughter, I would teach her that she is the daughter of a *King* and that she is *His* princess. If I had a daughter, I would teach her that she would make her own mistakes and that even she is sinful. If I had a daughter, I would teach her about the grace and mercy of God so that she, too, can enter the kingdom of heaven. If I had a daughter, I would teach her the value of a good husband because she is priceless. If I had a daughter, I would teach her how to be a wife to her husband. If I had daughter, I could only hope that I had a big enough influence in her life so she could teach her daughter the same things. I don't know if I will ever have a daughter, but if I did, I would want her to know I have already thought about her.

I don't know if I will ever have children of my own. I don't even know if I am physically able to make it through the whole process. But if I ever have a daughter of my own or if she is adopted, I would want her to know that this is for her.

> How precious are your thoughts about me, O God. They cannot be numbered! (Psalm 139:17)

If I Had a Son

April 18, 2016

If I had a son, I would want him to have a father he could look up to. If I had a son, I would want him to have a father as his role model. If I had a son, I would want him to learn how to be a man of God. If I had a son, I would teach him how to cook so he could cook for his wife. If I had a son, I would teach him how to pray so that he would be an example of Christ to his family. If I had a son, I would teach him that money is not everything and that it takes more than just money to provide for his family. If I had a son, I would tell him how important it is to be present in his family and that work is not the only thing that matters. If I had a son, I would teach him that drugs and alcohol are never the answer to his anger or his problems because when you are sober, you will have the same problems, if not bigger ones, before he got drunk. If I had a son, I would teach him how to love his wife and how to cherish her like his treasure. If I had a son, I would tell him that he belongs to God and that he is a prince of the living God. If I had a son, I could only hope that he would remember these lessons and teach them to his family. If I had a son, I would love to show him this one day.

This is for my future son, if I ever have one.

I don't know if I will, but just in case I do, I want him to know that I have already thought about him.

> Direct your children onto the right path,
> and when they are older, they will not leave it.
> (Proverbs 22:6)

Before I move on and talk about something else, I need to say something first. I just spent the last two pages talking about children I don't have. Yes, I thought about what it might be like to have kids, but I'm not sitting here writing about them because I am sad. God has allowed me to do many things because I don't have children. I've been able to pour my life into kids who need a friend, a mentor, a safe place, and a whole lot of love and hugs. I also have been that person who parents leave their kids with because they know they can trust me, and I will take extremely good care of them and love them. There is a lot to be said for that!

It gives me a chance to take care of someone I would not normally get to have, and Mom and Dad get a break. Sometimes I think that's God's way of saying, "I am giving you children of all ages who need you and want you, and they will also see me in you!" I don't take this lightly, and when I tell you I will love them, I really will. I may never have children of my own, but I will always treat yours as if they were mine.

Child of God

May 2, 2016

I am still just a kid, but no matter how old I get, I will always be a child. How does that work? When I accepted Christ, I became a child of God. I am a child of God. His blood runs through my veins. God chose me before I chose him. When you have a baby on the way, you don't have to think about loving that child. You love your child even before they have a chance to love you. The baby/child has done nothing to earn their parent's love. All of this works the same way with God's children. I am a child of God, and I am no longer a slave to sin. I have a Father even though I am fatherless, and He took my fears then replaced them with perfect love. He parted the water just so I could walk through the sea. I have already won the battles in my life with my Father beside me. I am a child of God, and I will never be taken out of His hands.

When I wrote this, it gave me a sense of security because even though I don't have my earthly father around me, this reminds me that my heavenly Father will never abandon me. It also tells me that nothing can take me away from Him.

> The Lord will not abandon his people, because that would dishonor his great name. For it has pleased the Lord to make you his very own people. (1 Samuel 12:22)

> My sheep listen to my voice; I know them, and they follow me. I give them eternal life, and they will never perish. No one can snatch them

away from me, for my Father has given them to me, and he is more powerful than anyone else. No one can snatch them from the Father's hand. (John 10:27–29)

Even if my father and mother abandon me, the Lord will hold me close. (Psalm 27:10)

More Than One Kind of Mom

May 8, 2016

Having a mom is important. You don't need biological child to be a mother. Biological mothers are not the only ones that matter. What about spiritual mothers? They are the ones who have the ability to teach another girl about who she is in Christ and how to live a godly life without coming across too strongly. What about those mothers who adopt you and treat you as their own even though they are not the ones who gave birth to you? They are the ones that you can talk to about anything and everything, and you know that they love you enough to tell you when you're doing something wrong. They are also the ones that you sometimes might find yourself being closer to than your biological mothers, and they can also see things in this child, good and bad, that sometimes the biological moms can't see. Whether you are a biological mom or not, you have probably been a mom to someone you didn't know needed another mom. Personally, I have divorced parents, which means my biological mom was a single mom for most of my life. I am the one who needed and still needs more than one mom. I have a spiritual mom. I have adoptive moms who have taken me in and do *everything* they can to love and protect me with everything they've got. You are a mom even when you don't think you are! There is more than one kind of mom!

To that single mom who can feel alone and overwhelmed, I wrote this for you. For the women who can never have children of their own, I feel for you. For that child whose mother left, I cry with you. If you have a special person who is like a mom to you, go love on her and tell her thank you. To those spiritual moms who spend so much time investing in our walk with Christ, love us enough to call us out and hold us when we cry. Words are not enough to thank you. You help us become the person God wants us to be, and there will never be enough words to express how thankful we are. For that mother who adopted children, you are amazing! You gave someone a home and a family that is safe, loving, and permanent. Thank you for taking someone and willingly calling them yours! You are living one of my dreams! For all those women who just flat-out love kids, I want you to know that you are appreciated! We need more people like you in this world!

This was written on May 8, 2016. It was on the Mother's Day weekend.

Happy Mother's Day!

> When she speaks, her words are wise, and she gives instructions with kindness. She carefully watches everything in her household and suffers nothing from laziness. (Proverbs 31:26–27)

Undefeated

May 16, 2016

All your life, you hear the words "Don't give up," but that is so much easier said than done. I have never been one to give up on anything, but there are many times I have felt defeated from every angle. I have been compared to other people and had the bar raised so high that I couldn't reach it. People think they are better than me because of money and their age, but then they find out I have lived through more than they could ever think. After fighting the words people say, climbing a mountain that never ends, and doing everything you can just to live in this world, the words "Don't give up" don't mean anything. I have been defeated, and I have fallen many times. Why have I chosen to stand when I know I can fall? Pure determination, heart, and knowing what I feel is temporary. Not only that, but every time I fall, I can choose to get back up. And the fact I have made it this far should persuade me to stand. Only when you choose to not get back up are you defeated. When you choose to get back up, that is how you become undefeated.

> Give your burdens to the Lord, and he will take care of you. He will not permit the godly to slip and fall. (Psalm 55:22)

> And endurance develops strength of character, and character strengthens our confident hope of salvation. (Romans 5:4)

The Living Word

May 26, 2016

Some people see the Holy Bible as just a book or words on a page or even a history book, but it is much more than that. None of these titles are right. The Holy Bible is the living word of God, and God breathed every word. It truly is holy. The word *holy* means "to be set apart or separated out." It is not dead; it is alive. It is everything to me, and it is not just words on a page. We should be so desperate for it that it should be like breathing. But instead, we take it for granted. And if we are lucky, you might open it once a week. The living word of God tells me my true value, my full potential, and my true destiny. I can't live without it. When everything falls apart, it should be the one thing we always stand on. The living word should be so obvious in us that we look alive, not dead!

What does the Bible mean to you?

> In the beginning the Word already existed. The Word was with God, and the Word was God. He existed in the beginning with God. God created everything through him, and nothing was created except through him. The Word gave life to everything that was created, and his life brought light to everyone. The light shines in the darkness, and the darkness can never extinguish it. (John 1:1–5)

The Life of a Babysitter

June 8, 2016

In one of my earlier blog entries, I talked about the life of a missionary. In this blog entry, I am going to share with you the life of a babysitter. I, for one, love to keep children, toddlers, and my favorite, babies! I started babysitting around the age of nine or ten. Babysitting and being a caregiver were two of the few things that came naturally to me. I never had to work at it. The life of a babysitter for me looks something like this.

You are able to stay completely calm with a screaming baby when the parent is having a meltdown. You have changed *so* many diapers that you are immune to the smell, and if you get pee on you, it doesn't bother you. If you are watching toddlers, you probably have the TV shows memorized. If they are coloring or doing crafts, you end up wanting to do it just as much. You are able to fix a bottle in less than two minutes *and* do it with one hand! You know their schedule just as well as the parents. You know all the safety hazards, you kiss boo-boos, you read stories at nap time, and you love on them just as much as their parents do.

I have done bath time, bedtime, and everything in between. I love sharing smiles, hugs, and laughter. Just knowing that they love me just as much as I love them makes it all worthwhile. Parents know they can trust me and that I will always be someone they can look up to. I don't look at babysitting as just a way to earn extra money. I treat every kid like they are mine because I may not be able to have one of my own, which makes me treasure it even more. So next time you are babysitting, don't complain. Look at it as a chance to love someone that may need extra love, be a positive role model, and truly embrace the life of a babysitter.

Being a babysitter takes patience, grace, and a love for children. I truly enjoy it, and the fact that I can put someone at ease when they leave their baby with me always makes me feel good just as a person. I don't take trust for granted because it is hard to earn and easy to lose. We should all be more careful with trust.

I do hope this made you laugh or at least smile today.

> Pure and genuine religion in the sight of God the Father means caring for orphans and widows in their distress and refusing to let the world corrupt you. (James 1:27)

> A gossip goes around telling secrets, but those who are trustworthy can keep a confidence. (Proverbs 11:13)

What Would You Do?

June 25, 2016

What would you do for twenty dollars? Would you wash a car? Would you cut grass? Walk dogs? Clean houses? What would you do for a penny? Would you wash that car, cut the grass, walk that dog, or clean that house? Chances are you probably would not do that for a penny. We treat people the same way without even realizing it. We treat some like they are worth our time and effort and then pass by others like they are worth nothing—like they are a penny. We can know a person our entire life and not know a thing about them, but it is only because we pass right by them. We should not treat people like they are at a certain level of importance. We have no right to pick and choose who is worth our twenty dollars and who is worth a penny. The people in your life should not have to guess what they are worth to you. Make sure they know the answer before they think they are worth nothing.

As humans, we like to place a value on everything. We put a value on almost everything we own. When we sell something, we automatically want to know how much it's worth and what we can get out of it. If we are not careful, we can treat people the same way.

As Christians, we are called to put others before ourselves. We should treat others how we want to be treated. I should feed you before I feed myself. All too often, we can have a tendency to put ourselves above others as if we are better than they are. We are not better than anyone, and we are not entitled to have everything someone else has.

Jesus did not pass by you and see you as a penny when you needed him. He saw you as a beautiful creation, and you were worth

Jesus dying on the cross. This is how we should see people because everybody is worth something to God.

> Yet God has made everything beautiful for its own time. He has planted eternity in the human heart, but even so, people cannot see the whole scope of God's work from beginning to end. (Ecclesiastes 3:11)

How God Used a Teenager

July 5, 2016

I have questions and comments constantly thrown at me. One of the questions I get asked is "How old are you?" and no one ever believes me when I tell them my real age. Most people think I'm about fifteen years old. Another question I get asked is "What can you possibly accomplish at your age?" I am only twenty years old, but I used most of my teenage years to change the world. This is how God can use a teenager.

At the age of thirteen, I started local missions. At the age of fourteen, I saved money for a girls' home in Thailand so they could have ice cream for the first time. I also coached an Upward soccer team. By the age of fifteen, I was mentoring, teaching special needs children karate, and teaching pre-K at my school. By the age of sixteen, I started speaking and traveling for global missions, and I did one of my biggest mission projects yet. When I was seventeen, I was saving to go on a mission trip to Thailand. By the time I was eighteen, I graduated from high school, left the country for my mission trip to Thailand, and started my training to preach/speak in churches in my district. I am the youngest person on record. When I turned nineteen, I started this blog, started a mission house in my own backyard shed, collected 150 Build-A-Bears for the local children's hospitals, and started writing my first book, *Angel in Disguise*.

This is how God used a teenager. Is this rare? Yes, it is, but it doesn't have to be! I'm not sure why He chose me, but what I do know is that God used somebody that was considered a weaker vessel to be the stronger one and to make the kingdom of God bigger. Not only did He use a teenager, but He also used a special needs teenager. Do not discount your youth!

If you're a teenager and you want to make a difference in the world, this is for you! God does not have an age requirement. If you want to and are willing to serve Him, He will use you! Don't let people get to you. Grow a backbone, be strong, and go for it!

The world needs more people like you!

> Don't let anyone think less of you because you are young. Be an example to all believers in what you say, in the way you live, in your love, your faith, and your purity. (1 Timothy 4:12)

1 Corinthians 13 (The Love Chapter)

July 23, 2016

As human beings, we long to be loved. Love can be misunderstood in so many different ways because we all want to be shown love differently. I don't want to focus so much on all the different love languages, but I would like to point out what the Bible says about love. First Corinthians 13 focuses on nothing but love. It is also known as the "love chapter." It is also used a lot in weddings. I want to take another look at it because there is so much more behind this chapter that we don't always see.

> If I speak in the tongues of men or of angels, but do not have love, I am only a resounding gong or a clanging cymbal. If I have the gift of prophecy and can fathom all mysteries and all knowledge, and if I have a faith that can move mountains, but do not have love, I am nothing. If I give all I possess to the poor and give over my body to hardship that I may boast, but do not have love, I gain nothing.
>
> Love is patient, love is kind. It does not envy, it does not boast, it is not proud. It does not dishonor others, it is not self-seeking, it is not easily angered, it keeps no record of wrongs. Love does not delight in evil but rejoices with the truth. It always protects, always trusts, always hopes, always perseveres.

Love never fails. But where there are prophecies, they will cease; where there are tongues, they will be stilled; where there is knowledge, it will pass away. For we know in part and we prophesy in part, but when completeness comes, what is in part disappears. When I was a child, I talked like a child, I thought like a child, I reasoned like a child. When I became a man, I put the ways of childhood behind me. For now we see only a reflection as in a mirror; then we shall see face to face. Now I know in part; then I shall know fully, even as I am fully known.

And now these three remain: faith, hope and love. But the greatest of these is love.

This clearly states what love is, but the Bible also says God is love.

Whoever does not *love* does not know *God*, because *God is love*. (1 John 4:8; emphasis added)

Now I am going to take 1 Corinthians 13 and replace the word *love* with *God*. It looks something like this:

If I speak in the tongues of men or of angels, but do not have *God*, I am only a resounding gong or a clanging cymbal. If I have the gift of prophecy and can fathom all mysteries and all knowledge, and if I have a faith that can move mountains, but do not have *God*, I am nothing. If I give all I possess to the poor and give over my body to hardship that I may boast, but do not have *God*, I gain nothing.

God is patient, *God* is kind. He does not envy, *He* does not boast, *He* is not proud. *He* does not dishonor others, *He* is not self-seeking, *He* is not easily angered, *He* keeps no record of wrongs. *God* does not delight in evil but rejoices with the truth. *He* always protects, always trusts, always hopes, always perseveres *God* never fails. But where there are prophecies, they will cease; where there are tongues, they will be stilled; where there is knowledge, it will pass away. For we know in part and we prophesy in part, but when completeness comes, what is in part disappears. When I was a child, I talked like a child, I thought like a child, I reasoned like a child. When I became a man, I put the ways of childhood behind me. For now we see only a reflection as in a mirror; then we shall see face to face. Now I know in part; then I shall know fully, even as I am fully known.

And now these three remain: faith, hope and *God*. But the greatest of these is *God*. (emphasis added)

This pretty much says it all.

If we don't have God, we have nothing.

Everything we are, everything we have, and everything I am is because of God.

A Letter for the Teacher

July 28, 2016

Dear schoolteacher,

Are you ready? Are you ready for another opportunity to impact and change the world? Whether you love or hate teaching, you have a chance to impact the world around you. The kids that walk into your room every day look up to you. Some will make you wonder why you started teaching in the first place. Others will love you and remind you why you started teaching. I have met teachers that love their jobs, but I have also met the ones who just do it for a paycheck. I was always able to tell the difference even if it was not my teacher. I am blessed to say that my teachers were amazing, and I was one of the kids that made teachers love their job no matter what grade I was in. My teachers helped me because I helped them. My teachers played a significant part in my life in and out of school.

Some kids will challenge you, and some kids will love you. But either way, they are watching you. They are watching how you come in through the door in the morning, how you look at hardship in life, and how you respond to each of them. And if you have any that were like me, you will have some that are waiting on you to wrap their arms around them. Teaching is not always about meeting state standards or benchmark test scores. Teaching is setting an example of integrity and not letting your bad days get to you. Your kids will look to you to help them reach their goals. If you give up on them, they will give up on themselves.

I wrote this at the beginning of the 2016–2017 school year. I wrote this as a letter for schoolteachers specifically. Whether you agree with me or not, everything I said is true. I have seen it, heard it, and watched it all with my own eyes. If you're a schoolteacher, please don't look over this and ignore it. You really can change the world. It's just a matter of whose world you're changing and how you're changing it. Are you changing someone's world in a positive way or a negative way? If you're teaching just for a paycheck, you need to get a new job. I'm not trying to sound harsh, but it's true. If you're doing it just for that, you most likely are bitter, angry, complain a lot, yell at your class all day long, and never get involved in a positive way. If you are this kind of teacher, then the only thing your students will remember is the negative things you did and said to them.

This can change someone's life, just not in the way you meant to.

If you're a teacher who teaches because you love kids and because you have a heart for young minds, you're in the right business! I strongly encourage you to teach with humility, integrity, kindness, and a heart that never runs out of love. These things cannot be taught by textbooks. They can only be taught by example. We cannot expect kids or, really, anyone, to be humble, honest, and kind if we are not willing to be this way ourselves. We have to practice what we preach; otherwise, it does no good for anyone. All parts of school are important, but don't think for one minute that the compassion you show is overlooked. The kids may not recognize you right then, but they will remember you for it later.

I know I did.

> If you need wisdom, ask our generous God,
> and he will give it to you. He will not rebuke you
> for asking. (James 1:5)

A Letter for the Student

August 7, 2016

Dear student,

Are you ready to work hard and set and achieve goals? It's a new school year, and you have a chance to make something great come out of it. Whether you are just starting school or going into a new grade, you have a chance to make something new. You have a voice, and it matters! If you see bullying in your school, be the one to make it stop. If you are a C student and you *know* you can make As, then make this school year the year you make the honor roll. If you see a teacher struggling through their day, be the one to help them. If you are like me in school where you try as hard as you can but hardly ever make the honor roll, use your strength and determination to power through and inspire others. Use this school year to encourage, not discourage. Be a role model, set goals for yourself, and reach them! Do your homework, study for your tests, turn in you projects and papers on time, and make sure you don't miss the bus! You can do it!

I believe you *are* ready!

Dear student,

I wrote this in the 2016–2017 school year. This was written to encourage you. In my heart of hearts, I want you to do your best. But I also know what it's like to be pushed too hard. Every school year, you have a chance to make a new version of yourself. Make the best of it! You can do it!

I know you can!

Do not be afraid or discouraged, for the Lord will personally go ahead of you. He will be with you; he will neither fail you nor abandon you. (Deuteronomy 31:8)

I know the Lord is always with me. I will not be shaken, for he is right beside me. (Psalm 16:8)

My Best Friend

August 22, 2016

I have lots of friends. I have friends that are like family and know me better than anyone. Then there's the best friend. A best friend is someone you do everything with, and you go through anything and everything together. When I was younger, I had what I thought were best friends, but then they would always turn out to be a fake. And I always got the short end of the stick. Today I have a best friend, but He is a little different from most. You may know Him. I can go in His house any time. He is even making me my own room! He stays awake with me when I am awake, and He is always up for conversation. He keeps me company when I am alone and never turns away. We go everywhere together! We go to church, sing songs, and ride in the car together. He protects me so I don't get hit. He provides for all my needs and even gives me some of my wants and desires. He makes me laugh and smile for no reason at all. He is awesome! Do you know my best friend? His name is Jesus! Do you know Him? If you don't, you should get to know Him because He is the best friend you are ever going to have.

I was so excited when I wrote this. It just made me feel like I could not be any closer to Jesus. Even as I think about it now, I feel so peaceful because it reminds me that I am never alone even when I feel alone. We all need friends and people that we can be close to, but Jesus it the only friend you can have that knows you and everything about you before you were even born.

He is your first best friend.

Such wicked people are detestable to the Lord, but he offers his friendship to the godly. (Proverbs 3:32)

Fingerprints of God

August 31, 2016

Many times, we underestimate God and who He is. We put God in a box and often think He is only for the rich or those wrapped nicely in a bow. We look for God in all the wrong places. God is seen in places we don't go or in people we never look at. He is in the weak, the poor, and the broken and abandoned that we ignore and look past. He is in the orphans and the fatherless. These are all places we never look. I have seen the poor, the weak, the broken and abandoned, the orphans, and the fatherless. The fingerprints of God were all over each of them. For years, I was considered weak, but today, that is not what is seen. God is not in a box. He could be right under your nose, but it's up to you to look for the fingerprints of God. Be careful if you use Windex because you just might wipe them off.

> May your ways be known throughout the earth, your saving power among people everywhere. (Psalm 67:2)

A Place in This World

September 11, 2016

There are times I can't help but wonder if I have a place in this world. I'm not talking about conforming to the world but just having a place where I fit and function like everyone else. People can say the nicest things to you or ask how you're doing, but you know they don't really care just by the tone of their voice. They only ask to make conversation. I try so hard just to get people's attention, but they won't even look me in the eye and actually talk to my face. Cerebral palsy can already make you feel like the odd one out because you work ten times harder to do normal functions, but then I hear people complain about the simplest things. Yet you never hear me say a word. I am a fighter, writer, missionary, speaker, babysitter, volunteer, role model, and mentor. I have tried every way possible to find a place in this world, but I never seem to fit in people's lives. Do people like me have a place in this world? If you say yes, then please help me find it. Your world and my world are two very different things, but I guarantee you, if you stop looking at what I don't have compared to you, then you will see I have all I will ever need.

My place in this world could be right in the middle of your heart.

I have gone through times where I feel totally lost in this world. This is a very strange feeling to me. It feels like you want to give up, but in your heart, you know you can't. So you keep walking through life anyway. Most people I know will probably be surprised when they read this because I don't discuss this part of my life much. As time has gone on, one of the things I have found helpful for myself is to stop living for the approval of people and stop trying to please others. I have learned to let people take me as I am. I should not have to have a certain kind of job, the right amount of money, a car, or a house to have a place in this world.

I am giving myself permission to be honest, and I give you the same permission if you have ever felt this way too.

You will never find your place in this world if you are following someone else's road map.

> There is more than enough room in my Father's home. If this were not so, would I have told you that I am going to prepare a place for you? (John 14:2)

Life Is a Highway

September 18, 2016

I spend a lot of time on the road. There are times I feel like my life is a highway. Every day, I go somewhere different, and I love it! Even though I do get tired sometimes, the people I meet are awesome, and I get to see a lot of places and help people. These are some of my favorite things. Sometimes I can't help but think like this.

Life is a highway. I wanna ride it all night long. If I'm going God's way, He's gonna drive it all night long. Through all these cities and all these towns, it's in my blood and it's all around. There's no load I can't hold. The road's so rough this I know. I'll be there when the light comes in, just tell 'em I'm a survivor. Life is a highway. I wanna ride it all night long. If I'm going God's way, He's gonna drive it all night long. There was a distance between him and me, a misunderstanding once, but now I can look the world straight in the eye. Life is a highway. I wanna ride it all night long. If I'm going God's way, He's gonna drive it all night long. (Words inspired by original song, "Life Is a Highway" by Rascal Flatts.)

Your word is a lamp to guide my feet and a
light for my path. (Psalm 119:105)

I Believe

September 30, 2016

If someone asked you what you believe in, what would you say? The Bible says to be ready to give an answer when someone asks you that. I don't know what your answer would be, but here is mine.

I believe in God the Father. I believe in Christ the Son. I believe in the Holy Spirit. My God is Three in One. I believe in the resurrection and that I will rise again. I believe in the name of Jesus! I believe that He is my judge and my defender, and I know that there is forgiveness in the name of Jesus! He came into the darkness to be the light. This I believe. I believe Jesus Christ is *Lord*! This will forever be my answer.

What is yours?

> But in your hearts revere Christ as Lord. Always be prepared to give an answer to everyone who asks you to give the reason for the hope that you have. But do this with gentleness and respect. (1 Peter 3:15)

Big Blue Eyes

October 16, 2016

I have big blue eyes. My big blue eyes see many things. They see broken hearts, smiles on faces, and everything else around them. The eyes are the windows to a person's soul or heart. You can be the best person at hiding what you really feel, but at some point, it will always come out though your actions, the expressions on your face, or your eyes. Everything I have seen with my big blue eyes is from the outside looking in. With that being said, I must ask this question. If you are on the outside looking into my life, what do you see? If you were to look straight into my eyes, what would you see? Even if you don't know me personally, you'd see my picture every time you read my blog. Even if you have never met me, you read my blogs, which means you have gotten to know me quite well. You have probably gotten to know me better than some because sometimes, I can write what I know better than trying to speak it. What do you see from the outside looking in?

On my blog website, there is a picture of me on my home page. I only have it there so that people who don't know me can have some idea of what I look like.

Even if you have never met me or know me at all, you have gotten to know me throughout this book or any other books I have written. One of my hopes is that when people read my books, they will find that they are not like most books. I like to be personal with people as if we were having a whole conversation by ourselves. I also hope that you or someone else gets to the end of my books and that it really does feel like we have met each other. As you read this book, what do you see, hear, or think about as you go through the pages? What sticks out the most?

I can only hope that my life reflects Jesus. That is my lifelong goal in everything I do. I can't do it without him, and I never plan to.

> Commit everything you do to the Lord. Trust him, and he will help you. (Psalm 37:5)

> Work willingly at whatever you do, as though you were working for the Lord rather than for people. (Colossians 3:23)

> In the same way, let your good deeds shine out for all to see, so that everyone will praise your heavenly Father. (Matthew 5:16)

Hooked on Jesus

October 26, 2016

Some people are addicted to drugs. Some people are addicted to alcohol. Some people are addicted to pornography or even food. You can be addicted to almost anything. For most people, it only takes one time before they are hooked, and a habit starts to form. I have never been addicted to anything, but I am definitely hooked on something. I am hooked on Jesus. Some symptoms might include singing praise and worship songs extremely loud, uncontrollable laughter or crying, unexplainable actions, and praying all throughout the day. This is the best addiction you could ever have. This addiction saves lives. It doesn't take them. These are good habits, not bad ones. This is the only thing I ever want to be addicted to. It is the best drug ever. It can heal anything and does not cost a thing.

> But let all who take refuge in you rejoice; let them sing joyful praises forever. Spread your protection over them, that all who love your name may be filled with joy. (Psalm 5:11)

Angel in Disguise

November 3, 2016

All right, so there has been a lot of uproar lately about book a called *Angel in Disguise*. I am super excited to say that this is the title of my first book! I am also very grateful for the amazing response it has gotten so far. This blog tells the story behind the story.

How did this book happen? To be honest, I'm still amazed that it actually did happen. I never thought I would ever have a book or even plan to write another one. When I was in school, I hated writing even though I wrote good papers. Now I spend every spare moment writing something new, and I love doing it! How does that work? I'm not sure. I have never seen God provide for me in the way that He has for this book. When I was writing it, I actually quit my job right in middle of preparing to find a publisher. I had to quit my job for many reasons, one of those reasons being that it wore me out so much that I was not physically functioning like I should, and I stayed sick all the time. I also quit because I knew I was not supposed to be there. I felt like there had to be something bigger. Well, I put my faith in action and trusted God with my life in a much bigger way than I ever have. I started doing local mission projects every month while taking professional speech classes and doing any work that God gave me, and it was always exactly what I needed, if not more. Today, because I stayed faithful, He gave me an amazing publisher who worked with me no matter what and walked me through the whole process from start to finish. She is a Christian and publishes nothing but Christian authors. He gave me work that covered *all* my expenses for this book plus more.

This sounds great and all, but I must say, I was put through a test before this happened. I was given the opportunity that sounded wonderful, but after asking for wisdom and knowing that I wanted to honor God with the story He gave me, this "wonderful opportunity" was not so wonderful. It did not honor God at all, so I turned it down. Instead, I was given an amazing person that honors God with her life. But this only happened after I passed the test right in front of me. After months of hard work and *lots* of patience, today you are able to read the story God gave me called *Angel in Disguise*. This is only the beginning! I am a dreamer who wants to *live* her dreams. God does provide when your intentions are to glorify him in all that you do!

This is the book title I am most known for. *Angel in Disguise* is the first book I ever wrote. I was nineteen years old when I wrote it, and my life has never been the same since. This book has gone far and wide around the world, and I still give God all the credit. *Angel in Disguise* is one half of my life story. I still have one half of my life to write about, which I have never made public. But until it's time, you are actually reading my published journal. My personal goal in this part of my life is to show you through my life that you are a valuable, beautiful, purposeful masterpiece of God. This book will walk you through a delicate portion of my life and show you how I came to learn this lesson myself.

After you finish this book, go find my very first book. I poured my heart into it.

You won't regret it, and you will never forget it.

Humble yourselves before the Lord, and he will lift you up in honor. (James 4:10)

Even strong young lions sometimes go hungry, but those who trust in the Lord will lack no good thing. (Psalm 34:10)

The Good Shepherd

November 19, 2016

In this day and age, there are no shepherds or sheep to herd, but that does not mean it never happened? Sheep are still animals, but they are not everywhere like they were in the past. Have you ever thought about a shepherd and a sheep? Or what the job of a shepherd is? A shepherd herds sheep together so they don't just wander into a field that is not fit for them. A shepherd also protects his flock from the wolves so that they don't get attacked or eaten. The sheep are so well trained that they know the sound of the shepherd's voice even if he is talking to only one.

A shepherd's job is not easy. Shepherds stay out in the hot sun for hours just to keep watch over each sheep. Many shepherds carry staffs to help redirect the sheep if they wander away. Even though shepherds are not common like they were, there is still one shepherd that never stops protecting his sheep. He is called the Good Shepherd.

I am a sheep. How am I a sheep? I am in a herd of many believers to help me not wander away from my shepherd. I have also been protected from wolves that could have killed me. I have been redirected by the staff (the Word) of my shepherd when I wander away. But importantly, I hear my shepherd's voice and what He really thinks of me. My shepherd loves me and takes care of me. I can only know that because I am one of His sheep.

Are you a sheep who knows the Good Shepherd?

"I tell you the truth, anyone who sneaks over the wall of a sheepfold, rather than going through the gate, must surely be a thief and a robber! But the one who enters through the gate is the shepherd of the sheep. The gatekeeper opens the gate for him, and the sheep recognize his voice and come to him. He calls his own sheep by name and leads them out. After he has gathered his own flock, he walks ahead of them, and they follow him because they know his voice. They won't follow a stranger; they will run from him because they don't know his voice."

Those who heard Jesus use this illustration didn't understand what he meant, so he explained it to them: "I tell you the truth, I am the gate for the sheep. All who came before me were thieves and robbers. But the true sheep did not listen to them. Yes, I am the gate. Those who come in through me will be saved. They will come and go freely and will find good pastures. The thief's purpose is to steal and kill and destroy. My purpose is to give them a rich and satisfying life.

"I am the good shepherd. The good shepherd sacrifices his life for the sheep. A hired hand will run when he sees a wolf coming. He will abandon the sheep because they don't belong to him and he isn't their shepherd. And so the wolf attacks them and scatters the flock. The hired hand runs away because he's working only for the money and doesn't really care about the sheep.

"I am the good shepherd; I know my own sheep, and they know me, just as my Father knows me and I know the Father. So I sacrifice my life for the sheep. I have other sheep, too, that are not in this sheepfold. I must bring them also. They will listen to my voice, and there will be one flock with one shepherd.

"The Father loves me because I sacrifice my life so I may take it back again. No one can take my life from me. I sacrifice it voluntarily. For I have the authority to lay it down when I want to and also to take it up again. For this is what my Father has commanded." (John 10:1–18)

Dressed in White

November 27, 2016

One day, I can't wait to be dressed in white. One day, I will walk down the aisle. I will look straight ahead and see my Father, who loves me. When I get to the end, I will look around and see all the people I have lost along the way. I will have a crown to lay at my Father's feet, and He will wipe away every tear I've ever cried then call me His daughter. Every pain I've ever felt will be gone. Wearing white never sounded so good, especially when you are entering the kingdom of heaven. For now, I can only dream about what it will be like. I have no doubt in my mind you thought I was talking about a wedding at the beginning, but that will not be the only time I will be dressed in white.

Heaven comes to my mind many times when I think about wearing white. Sometimes it makes me smile, and sometimes it makes me cry. Thinking about heaven gives me hope. Sometimes it can feel like my mind is already there. That's what makes this one unique, and my imagination runs wild. Heaven reminds me that this earthly life is not the be-all and end-all.

This earth is not made to be our permanent residence.

> All who are victorious will be clothed in white. I will never erase their names from the Book of Life, but I will announce before my Father and his angels that they are mine. (Revelation 3:5)

> He will wipe every tear from their eyes, and there will be no more death or sorrow or crying or pain. All these things are gone forever. (Revelation 21:4)

Mary, Did You Know?

December 16, 2016

If you could write a letter and send it back in time two thousand years, would you? If you could write a letter to Mary (the mother of Jesus) and tell her what her son has done for you, what would you say? If I could send a letter to Mary and tell her what her son has done for me, that would be so cool! If I could send a letter, this is what I would say.

Dear Mary,

My name is Rebecca Leatherwood, and I am from the future. You will never meet me, but I know exactly who you are. You carried the Savior of the whole world! I know that was scary for you and that you went through a lot just to deliver a baby. I just wanted to say thank you so much for choosing to bring Jesus into the world because if you didn't, I don't know what we would have done!

There is a song that was written about you called "Mary, Did You Know?" The truth is, you don't know. You don't know the impact your son has had on me. I have cerebral palsy. I know you don't know what that is, but basically, it changes how your whole body works. And sometimes you can't walk because of it. I'm not healed from it, but because of your son, Jesus, I can walk and do all kinds of things that people never thought I would be able to do. He put me through a lot to get here, but now I get to tell the story Jesus wrote for me. And now more people are going to heaven! Without Jesus, I would never smile or laugh, and most importantly, I would never get to go to heaven.

Mary, did you know that if you had a baby now, you could have it in a hospital? That is a place with a bed and lots of medical equipment to help take care of you and your baby. Yep, that's right! You would not have to find a place to have a baby. You definitely would not have to give birth on the ground, and you would not have to put your baby in a feed trough. I have been to the hospital a lot but not because I was having a baby. I can't even imagine what it was like seeing your son being crucified. I can't even describe how sorry I am that you had to watch that. Thank you for being the person you are and for thinking about all the people that would be saved because of your son. Without him, I would not even be able to write this.

I hope this letter makes you smile!

Love,
Rebecca Leatherwood

This is how Jesus the Messiah was born. His mother, Mary, was engaged to be married to Joseph. But before the marriage took place, while she was still a virgin, she became pregnant through the power of the Holy Spirit. (Matthew 1:18)

What Christmas Means to Me

December 24, 2016

I understand that Christmas was originally a pagan holiday. I understand that Jesus was not born on December 25. I understand that we as Christians are the ones that turned it into a Christian holiday. I understand that the Bible does not tell us to celebrate the birth of Jesus. I understand many other things about the history of Christmas. Here is what I don't understand. How can someone focus so much on the negative things about Christmas?

If I say I celebrate Christmas and you are offended, that means you have come to your own conclusions about Christmas and why I celebrate it. Please here me out.

Here is how I see it. I do celebrate Christmas, but you should look at the intentions of my heart before you form an opinion because this is what Christmas means to me. Christmas reminds me that God keeps His promises. God sent His Son to save us just like He promised. This is the best gift, and it was given for free and did not come wrapped in plastic. Christmas gives me a chance to give and bless someone just like Jesus gave His life for me, and now I have to give and bless someone else. The red lights remind me of the blood of Jesus, and the white reminds me that my sins have been washed away and that I have been made new. The green reminds me of my growth and walk with Jesus as I look back at all He has done for me. The gold reminds me of heaven and that I will one day live forever. Christmas for me is not about presents. Please don't misunderstand me; I do like to open presents, but it makes me think about how God continues to bless me even when I mess up. This is what Christmas means to me. These are the intentions of my heart.

It does not matter when you celebrate it or how. It only matters that you do.

> In the sixth month of Elizabeth's pregnancy, God sent the angel Gabriel to Nazareth, a village in Galilee, to a virgin named Mary. She was engaged to be married to a man named Joseph, a descendant of King David. Gabriel appeared to her and said, "Greetings, favored woman! The Lord is with you!"
>
> Confused and disturbed, Mary tried to think what the angel could mean, "Don't be afraid, Mary," the angel told her, "for you have found favor with God! You will conceive and give birth to a son, and you will name him Jesus. He will be very great and will be called the Son of the Most High. The Lord God will give him the throne of his ancestor David. And he will reign over Israel forever; his Kingdom will never end!"
>
> Mary asked the angel, "But how can this happen? I am a virgin."
>
> The angel replied, "The Holy Spirit will come upon you, and the power of the Most High will overshadow you. So the baby to be born will be holy, and he will be called the Son of God. What's more, your relative Elizabeth has become pregnant in her old age! People used to say she was barren, but she has conceived a son and is now in her sixth month. For the word of God will never fail."
>
> Mary responded, "I am the Lord's servant. May everything you have said about me come true." And then the angel left her. (Luke 1:26–38)

Work in Progress

January 8, 2017

I never claimed to be perfect. I never claimed to be finished or done. I am a work in progress. I am a never-ending construction zone. Every day, I want to strive to be what God wants me to be. I am a progression of work. I will never say that I know everything about God, and if I do, then that is a very dangerous place to be. We are all a work in progress even if you don't realize it. Every day, you work to make yourself better or make something better for yourself. You just don't always see it. Having a walk with God is also a work in progress, except it looks like this. It takes more than just patience and waiting for God to do something great in your life. It takes you! Every day, we should be trying, working, and striving to be what God wants us to be. You will never learn everything about God, but that doesn't mean you shouldn't try. That is why your spiritual journey is a work in progress. You will never be finished or done. You will never be perfect, but that is where God comes in. When God comes in our construction zone, it looks like this.

You need grace for yourself, and you need to make space for His work in you. As you progress, He is pro-grace. It's not just about the work. It's about allowing His amazing grace in your amazing race and never giving up in striving to be what God wants you to be. God is always working in your construction zone because He is never finished or done.

Even though I understand I am not perfect, I, too, make mistakes, and it is hard for me to give grace to myself.

It is a lot easier for me to have grace for others than it is to myself. This part of me will always be a work in progress, or should I say "pro-grace."

Are you like me?

Is it easier for you to have grace for others and not yourself?

> One who loves a pure heart and who speaks with grace will have the king for a friend. (Proverbs 22:11)

> The Word became flesh and made his dwelling among us. We have seen his glory, the glory of the one and only Son, who came from the Father, full of grace and truth. (John 1:14)

> Out of his fullness we have all received grace in place of grace already given. (John 1:16)

We Are the Church

February 12, 2017

I go to church. I go in a building with walls and doors. When I go to church, I see a cross hanging on the wall. I go to church to learn about God and the love of Jesus Christ, to worship, and to sing. What happens after that? What happens after you get up on Sunday morning and go through the motions of the "Christian walk"? Just because you might go to church does not mean you are a Christ follower. That is like walking into Burger King and saying, "I'm a hamburger." Having a personal relationship with Jesus Christ is a whole topic for a blog all by itself. This one is for the Church goers.

I go to church and learn about God. I study the Bible on my own and dig into the Word. I have knowledge most people don't have. What good is any of this if I'm not doing anything with it? What good does it do to go to church Sunday after Sunday and learn everything you can if you do nothing with what you have learned? What good is studying the Bible on your own if you don't act out what you believe? If you have the best gift from God, personally, why would you not want to share it with someone else? You can go to church all you want and know everything about God, but until you do something with what you have, it means nothing. Get outside of the building, walls, and doors and put what you say you believe into action! Share what you sing about and study about with someone else. A building with walls, doors, and crosses is *not* the church! We are the church! God told us to make disciples. That means we are to quickly spread His Word through our actions and our words. People make the church, not the building!

You may not realize this, and sometimes I even forget. When we accept Christ, our bodies become a temple for the Holy Spirit. That means Jesus lives in us. It also means our bodies become living sacrifices. We die to ourselves and become a part of the body of Christ. This is why we are the church of a living God.

It's not about a building or what's inside it; it's about what is inside us.

> Don't you realize that your body is the temple of the Holy Spirit, who lives in you and was given to you by God? You do not belong to yourself, for God bought you with a high price.
>
> So you must honor God with your body. (1 Corinthians 6:19–20)

> And so, dear brothers and sisters, I plead with you to give your bodies to God because of all he has done for you. Let them be a living and holy sacrifice the kind he will find acceptable. This is truly the way to worship him. Don't copy the behavior and customs of this world, but let God transform you into a new person by changing the way you think. Then you will learn to know God's will for you, which is good and pleasing and perfect. (Romans 12:1–2)

> Now, dear brothers and sisters, regarding your question about the special abilities the Spirit gives us. I don't want you to misunderstand this. You know that when you were still pagans, you were led astray and swept along in worshiping speechless idols. So I want you to know that no one speaking by the Spirit of God will curse Jesus, and no one can say Jesus is Lord, except by the Holy Spirit. (1 Corinthians 12:1–3)

Heart of a Lion

February 26, 2017

Lions are known as the king of the jungle. Lions lead the jungle. Lions are strong, and they have the attitude that shows courage, strength, and bravery. They have the strength to fight for their lives and for what they want. Do you have the attitude of a lion? The heart of a lion is this: having the strength and bravery to go in your own direction when others simply follow the herd, having the attitude that says, "I can and I will!" Your attitude is your altitude! Your attitude is what you think, what you do, and how you feel about yourself. Attitude is everything in life. Why? Because whether you rise or fall, your attitude is what's left over when you're finished. I have been through rough times, and I want you to know it was not my money that brought me this far! It was my attitude toward life! Yes, I did not always want to fight. Yes, it is hard. And I do cry sometimes, but I have to keep going because I want to attack the life I had and take back what's mine! That is the attitude of a lion!

What do you think of yourself? Do you think of yourself as how God thinks of you, or do you care more about what your friends and family think of you? You need the lion attitude that says, "I am bold enough to fight!" Be a lion! Be fearless! Stop talking and start walking! Real lions demonstrate who they are. They do not seek respect because they already have it. If I want something, I go after it with everything I have inside of me! There are no maybes with the lion. Don't let people push you around. Stand strong like the lion, and no one will question your goals again because a lion leads! You have the heart of a lion!

So then, since Christ suffered physical pain, you must arm yourselves with the same attitude he had, and be ready to suffer, too. For if you have suffered physically for Christ, you have finished with sin. (1 Peter 4:1)

Is Suffering Necessary?

March 15, 2017

What comes to your mind when you think about suffering? You might think about physical pain or emotional pain. We sometimes look at suffering like it is a competition, and we compare each other's circumstances. In other words, my pain is greater than yours. Then we discount the other person's physical or emotional pain like it has no value. I have cerebral palsy and scoliosis. To you, it may sound like I'm suffering, but to be honest, I was born with it. So I have no clue what it is like to live without it. So how can I be suffering if I don't know any other way of living? You have to remember that I was not always like this. I went from my worst condition to the best I can possibly be. Over time (and yes, I did suffer from physical and emotional pain), I have met many other kids with my same condition. Some were obviously worse than others, and I can't help but want to help them. If you watch me closely, I am always smiling when you see me. I could be hurting right in front of you, and you would never know. Why? The Bible says that suffering produces perseverance (Romans 5:3).

You know how it is: if you did not go through what you have gone through, you would not be who you are today. The definition of perseverance is "the steady persistence in a course of action, a purpose, a state, especially in spite of difficulties, obstacles, or discouragement" (www.dictionary.com). Do I think God could have thought of a better way for us to learn perseverance? *Yes!* I'm not saying I never cried or that I thought surgery was fun. One of the hardest things for me is to watch someone suffer, especially if it's someone who clearly does not deserve it.

Imagine living your life without suffering or having a life with no difficulties or obstacles. Some of you would love that, and I have met people who live like this yet are still missing something.

God is missing!

If you had the "perfect" life, you would have no reason to rely on God. Is suffering necessary? Yes. Why? Because without it, you would never turn to God, and you would never be who He made you to be.

> You have allowed me to suffer much hardship, but you will restore me to life again and lift me up from the depths of the earth. (Psalm 71:20)

One-Way Street

March 31, 2017

I am the kind of person that could get lost in a paper bag. I have no sense of direction, and I am the kind of person that needs landmarks, not a street name. The interstate terrifies me, and I really get frustrated if I miss a turn. Is anybody else like this? If you are, you would say, "*Amen!*" with everything inside you. I need a GPS! I am not afraid to say it! I am that person who can still get lost with a GPS.

I am so glad that walking with God is not like this. I don't need a GPS, road signs, or a map to get to God. Praise God because if I did, I don't know if I would make it! I don't have to turn right, turn left, or go in reverse just so I can turn around. I can go straight ahead, and I only have to go one way to get to God! The Bible says that Jesus is the only way to get to God and enter the kingdom of heaven. All too often, people think there are multiple ways to get to heaven when there is only one. You can't take interstates or different streets. You don't even need a GPS or a map. You may be lost in a paper bag and you probably have messed up in life and missed a turn, but there is good news! There is a new driver in town, and His name is God. He will take you down the one-way street named Jesus, and you will never be lost again.

> "No, we don't know, Lord," Thomas said. "We have no idea where you are going, so how can we know the way?"
>
> Jesus told him, "I am the way, the truth, and the life. No one can come to the Father except through me. If you had really known me, you would know who my Father is. From now on, you do know him and have seen him!" (John 14:5–7 NLT)

What Easter Means to Me

April 15, 2017

It's Easter weekend once again! Everywhere I look, I see Easter eggs, Easter bunnies, Easter candy, Easter baskets, and pastel colors. For Christmas this past year, I wrote a blog entry called "What Christmas Means to Me." Now I am going to tell you what Easter means to me.

Easter is yet again a pagan holiday. All the bunnies that you see in Walmart are left over from a pagan festival called Eostre. All the bunnies that you see come from a goddess whose symbol was a rabbit. Easter eggs are celebrated in many different cultures and have different meanings depending on the culture. What does all of this have to do with Jesus? Absolutely nothing! All of this might be fun, but if I think about what Easter means to me, it's really disappointing. Even though I understand all of this, I still celebrate Easter, but it has nothing to do with eggs, bunnies, or candy. Easter means much more than this. To me, Easter represents Passover, betrayal, crucifixion, and resurrection.

On a Friday, Jesus was betrayed, put on trial, beat, spit on, and handed over to the Roman soldiers to be crucified. His body was ripped apart, and every drop of His blood was poured out. After hanging on a cross for six hours, Jesus was dead, and He did what He was sent to do. He was sent to die so we one day might live. Jesus was then placed in a tomb with a stone rolled across the opening. Then Sunday came! The stone was rolled away, and sin, death, and the devil were defeated forever! All the prophecies that were ever told about Jesus came true just as God said, and life was given to all who believed! This is what Easter means to me. This is much more fulfilling than candy that melts, baskets that are plastic, bunnies that come from something false, and eggs that will break. I now have a home in heaven because of what happened over the Easter weekend. I have everlasting life because Jesus willingly gave His life.

Jesus Is Betrayed and Arrested

After saying these things, Jesus crossed the Kidron Valley with his disciples and entered a grove of olive trees. Judas, the betrayer, knew this place, because Jesus had often gone there with his disciples. The leading priests and Pharisees had given Judas a contingent of Roman soldiers and Temple guards to accompany him. Now with blazing torches, lanterns, and weapons, they arrived at the olive grove.

Jesus fully realized all that was going to happen to him, so he stepped forward to meet them. "Who are you looking for?" he asked.

"Jesus the Nazarene," they replied.

"I am he," Jesus said. (Judas, who betrayed him, was standing with them.) As Jesus said "I am he," they all drew back and fell to the ground! Once more he asked them, "Who are you looking for?"

And again they replied, "Jesus the Nazarene."

"I told you that I am he," Jesus said. "And since I am the one you want, let these others go." He did this to fulfill his own statement: "I did not lose a single one of those you have given me."

Then Simon Peter drew a sword and slashed off the right ear of Malchus, the high priest's slave. But Jesus said to Peter, "Put your sword back into its sheath. Shall I not drink from the cup of suffering the Father has given me?"

Jesus was then taken to the High Priest. Peter (a disciple of Jesus) denies Jesus three times. He was then put on trial before Pilate.

Jesus was then sentenced to death. (John 18)

Then Pilate had Jesus flogged with a lead-tipped whip. The soldiers wove a crown of thorns and put it on his head, and they put a purple robe on him. "Hail! King of the Jews!" they mocked, as they slapped him across the face.

Pilate went outside again and said to the people, "I am going to bring him out to you now, but understand clearly that I find him not guilty." Then Jesus came out wearing the crown of thorns and the purple robe. And Pilate said, "Look, here is the man!"

When they saw him, the leading priests and Temple guards began shouting, "Crucify him! Crucify him!"

"Take him yourselves and crucify him," Pilate said. "I find him not guilty."

The Jewish leaders replied, "By our law he ought to die because he called himself the Son of God."

When Pilate heard this, he was more frightened than ever. He took Jesus back into the headquarters again and asked him, "Where are you from?" But Jesus gave no answer. "Why don't you talk to me?" Pilate demanded. "Don't you realize that I have the power to release you or crucify you?"

Then Jesus said, "You would have no power over me at all unless it were given to you from above. So the one who handed me over to you has the greater sin."

Then Pilate tried to release him, but the Jewish leaders shouted, "If you release this man, you are no 'friend of Caesar.' Anyone who declares himself a king is a rebel against Caesar."

When they said this, Pilate brought Jesus out to them again. Then Pilate sat down on the judgment seat on the platform that is called the Stone Pavement (in Hebrew, Gabbatha). It was now about noon on the day of preparation for the Passover. And Pilate said to the people, "Look, here is your king!"

"Away with him," they yelled. "Away with him! Crucify him!"

"What? Crucify your king?" Pilate asked.

"We have no king but Caesar," the leading priests shouted back.

Then Pilate turned Jesus over to them to be crucified.

The Crucifixion

So they took Jesus away. Carrying the cross by himself, he went to the place called Place of the Skull (in Hebrew, Golgotha). There they nailed him to the cross. Two others were crucified with him, one on either side, with Jesus between them. And Pilate posted a sign on the cross that read, "Jesus of Nazareth,[d] the King of the Jews." The place where Jesus was crucified was near the city, and the sign was written in Hebrew, Latin, and Greek, so that many people could read it.

Then the leading priests objected and said to Pilate, "Change it from 'The King of the Jews' to 'He said, I am King of the Jews.'"

Pilate replied, "No, what I have written, I have written."

When the soldiers had crucified Jesus, they divided his clothes among the four of them. They also took his robe, but it was seamless, woven in one piece from top to bottom. So they said, "Rather than tearing it apart, let's throw dice[e] for it." This fulfilled the Scripture that says,

"They divided my garments among themselves and threw dice for my clothing." So that is what they did.

Standing near the cross were Jesus' mother, and his mother's sister, Mary (the wife of Clopas), and Mary Magdalene. When Jesus saw his mother standing there beside the disciple he loved, he said to her, "Dear woman, here is your son." And he said to this disciple, "Here is your mother." And from then on this disciple took her into his home.

The Death of Jesus

Jesus knew that his mission was now finished, and to fulfill Scripture he said, "I am thirsty." A jar of sour wine was sitting there, so they soaked a sponge in it, put it on a hyssop branch, and held it up to his lips. When Jesus had tasted it, he said, "It is finished!" Then he bowed his head and gave up his spirit.

It was the day of preparation, and the Jewish leaders didn't want the bodies hanging there the next day, which was the Sabbath (and a very special Sabbath, because it was Passover week). So they asked Pilate to hasten their deaths by ordering that their legs be broken. Then their bodies could be taken down. So the soldiers came and broke the legs of the two men crucified with Jesus. But when they came to Jesus, they saw that he was already dead, so they didn't break his legs.

One of the soldiers, however, pierced his side with a spear, and immediately blood and water flowed out. (This report is from an eyewitness giving an accurate account. He speaks the truth so that you also may continue to believe.) These things happened in fulfillment of the Scriptures that say, "Not one of his bones will be broken," and "They will look on the one they pierced."

The Burial of Jesus

Afterward Joseph of Arimathea, who had been a secret disciple of Jesus (because he feared the Jewish leaders), asked Pilate for permission to take down Jesus' body. When Pilate gave permission, Joseph came and took the body away. With him came Nicodemus, the man who had come to Jesus at night. He brought about seventy-five pounds of perfumed ointment made from myrrh and aloes. Following Jewish burial custom, they wrapped Jesus' body with the spices in long sheets of linen cloth. The place of crucifixion was near a garden, where there was a new tomb, never used before. And so, because it was the day of preparation for the Jewish Passover and since the tomb was close at hand, they laid Jesus there. (John 19)

The Resurrection

Early on Sunday morning, while it was still dark, Mary Magdalene came to the tomb and found that the stone had been rolled away from the entrance. She ran and found Simon Peter and the other disciple, the one whom Jesus loved. She said, "They have taken the Lord's body out of the tomb, and we don't know where they have put him!"

Peter and the other disciple started out for the tomb. They were both running, but the other disciple outran Peter and reached the tomb first. He stooped and looked in and saw the linen wrappings lying there, but he didn't go in. Then Simon Peter arrived and went inside. He also noticed the linen wrappings lying there, while the cloth that had covered Jesus' head was folded up and lying apart from the other wrappings. Then the disciple who had reached the tomb first also went in, and he saw and believed—for until then they still hadn't understood the Scriptures that said Jesus must rise from the dead. Then they went home. (John 20)

This is what Easter means to me.

What does it me to you knowing that Jesus went through all of this and more not only to save you but because he loves you?

A Servant's Heart

April 30, 2017

One of my favorite things to do is serve people. I enjoy being able to meet other people's needs and lend a helping hand. That is one of the reasons why I became a missionary. Some people might say I have a servant's heart, but what does that even mean? It could mean a number of things, but here is how I see it. Just because I say *servant* does not mean I am a slave to people. I say that because people think servant equals slave, and that's not always true. Let's think about motive. Why do I like to serve? It is said that it is a blessing to be a blessing. I enjoy seeing people smile when they discover that some part of their workday is already finished because I did their work when they were not looking. I enjoy being able to meet a need and take care of someone if they don't have something and I know I can take care of it. Last but not least, I love it when people hug me and tell me how much they appreciate it. I know that sounds simple, but it's true. Those are three very basic reasons of why serving people is one of my favorite things to do. But there is still a very deep reason why I love to serve others. The main motive I have for serving people really does not have anything to do with people at all. It may look like I am serving you, but I am really not. I am serving God, and you benefit from it. My main goal is to serve God, and that is also my true motive. If that's my true motive, then shouldn't I look like Jesus? Jesus washed His disciples' feet, and He did it willingly. He even put on the garment of a slave when He did it. He did this as an example for us. Not only did He do it willingly; He did it humbly.

This is why if you ever watch me serve, I can do it with joy and a smile and never do it to show off. I never get tired of serving because of who I am doing it for.

Have I ever felt taken advantage of? Yes! Have people ever questioned me? Yes!

Do I ever question myself? Yes! Do I ever feel like stopping? Yes! But I don't let any of these reasons stop me because I see the impact of it. And as far as the other people go, God will take care of them for me. It is very hard for me to think about myself, but that's a good problem to have.

A servant's heart is very fragile, but it is only because their heart breaks for people.

> Do to others whatever you would like them to do to you. This is the essence of all that is taught in the law and the prophets. (Matthew 7:12)

Voice of God

May 20, 2017

Have you ever heard God speak to you? Maybe you have or maybe you haven't, but how often do we miss it? God can use anything He wants to try to get our attention. He will do anything to get you to hear His voice. It breaks my heart to think about how many times I have missed it, but I also know how much it means to me when I can hear it loud and clear. Have you ever thought about what He could use to get your attention? Have you ever heard a worship song that set your spirit free? Have you ever watched the sun rise right in front of you and saw how beautiful it truly is? Have you ever cried tears that you could not explain? What if that was God right there in front of you? Have you ever lost a loved one who you thought should still be here? Have you ever met a stranger that already knew your name? Have you ever been tangled up in fear? How often do we miss these things? He speaks through it all, but we have to listen very carefully because it's usually very quiet. Who knows how He will get a hold of you to prove He is enough? Sometimes the only thing God wants to tell you is, *"I love you!"*

Are you going to be able to hear the voice of God tell you those three extremely valuable words through the busyness of your life?

The voice of the Lord is powerful; the voice
of the Lord is majestic. (Psalm 29:4)

Fighter inside Me

May 29, 2017

I am a fighter. I am determined, and at times, it might come across as me being stubborn. I mean this in the sweetest, most down-to-earth way. The more you tell me I can't do something, the more I am going to fight to accomplish whatever goal I have set out in front of me. Can you honestly blame me for fighting? I have cerebral palsy. Fighting has been in my blood since day 1. I was told I was never going to do anything with my life. What all those people did was add fuel to the fire. I have had five surgeries, learned how to walk three times, and have had many types of therapy just to learn how to make my body function. The list goes on forever, but my point is, I fought for my life when people told me that I shouldn't. This is the kind of fighter that lives inside me. I was also told I would never play sports. Today, I have played soccer and have a black belt in karate. I really do know how to fight, and I have also taught others to fight for themselves. I was born to fight, but it was only because I had no other choice. People fight against me, but they are only making the fire bigger. People make smart comments on how I live and how they think I will never have a job that amounts to anything. How is this true when you are constantly thinking of new ways to change the world? I am a speaker, a writer, and a missionary. God has given me the ability to change lives. I have been able to meet hundreds of people, and I have only scratched the surface. I fight against the negative words of others, my own physical body, my own thoughts, and other people's expectations of what they think I should be doing with my life. I am a fighter, and I have ambition, determination, and goals that live inside me. God gave me all these adjectives that could describe me. All these make the fighter that lives in me.

What words can you use to describe yourself, and how are they used to make up the person you are or are becoming?

> Fight the good fight for the true faith. Hold tightly to the eternal life to which God has called you, which you have declared so well before many witnesses. (1 Timothy 6:12)

Small-Town Hero

June 26, 2017

My name is Rebecca Leatherwood. I live in a small town in Georgia. I can go almost anywhere and know someone. I have gone to churches, stores, restaurants, the movies, and even banks and always manage to make a new friend, or I go in the same stores so much that I know the employees. Some people have even called me their hero. Why that is, I'm not exactly sure. But it makes me smile, so it's okay. You would be amazed at what a smile does and what a real conversion means to a cashier. That's how most people remember who I am. I have also been pulled aside by store employees and asked this question: "Do you have cerebral palsy?" I say yes, but how some of these people are able to spot it, I'm not always sure. What I do know is that when I leave, they smile back at me or give me a hug, and then I hear these words: "You're such an inspiration!" These words mean a lot, but I never thought of myself that way. To me, I'm just being myself because that's what I'm the best at. I don't feel like a hero, but if you can be someone's hero or inspiration by being yourself, that's awesome because you don't have to work at it. I'm Rebecca, and I'm someone's small-town hero just by being myself.

It took me my entire lifetime to get myself to the point of being so comfortable with being myself that I don't want to be anyone else. If there is one thing I have learned through caring for others, it's that most people want the authentic version of yourself. They do not want a fake person because there is already enough of that in the world. People are always drawn to "real people," but it's up to you what that looks like.

You have to be comfortable within yourself before you can be comfortable with others.

> And yet, O Lord, you are our Father. We are the clay, and you are the potter. We all are formed by your hand. (Isaiah 64:8)

All the Single Ladies

June 26, 2017

Can I be really honest for just a minute? I am single, and I have never dated anyone. Your brain probably just exploded on the inside. Yes! I am in my very early twenties, and I have never dated anyone. A lot of this has to do with the simple fact that I never had a big interest in dating. I missed out on a lot when I was younger, and now I am making up for it in the best way possible. The other reason is simple: I'm just not ready for it, and I am single by choice. I have been hit on many times, and I must say, it looks cheap. These are the top four things you should not say to a single person. This is just my personal opinion.

Do you have anyone in your life? I have been asked this so many times. People make it sound like I'm lonely, desperate, and have no other friends. Of course, I have people in my life! Seriously... I was recently asked this question. Here was my response. I smiled and laughed because I knew exactly what this person meant. I said, "It's just me and Jesus." This person was not expecting that for an answer!

1. "You have time!" Unless you know the future, you probably should not say that. People say that education is number 1, so most people my age are in school, working and chasing their dreams. My case is a little different. I took the missionary road and became a speaker and author at a very young age. Older people tell young people to focus on themselves. I am focused on God and the people He has put in front of me. How can you tell me I have time when we don't even know what tomorrow looks like?

2. "It will happen when you least expect it." I don't ever want to be at a place in life where I'm so focused on trying to

have a boyfriend that I miss out on the amazing things that God is doing right in front of me. I know that if I wait on God to send me that one person, then I won't have to second-guess the man He sent for me.

3. "You need to learn how to be content." I don't think it's good to tell someone to not pray for it or for that desire to be laid on their heart. "Well, maybe when you're content enough, God will send you someone." Who said you can't pray for the person you desire before you know them? Chances are they are going to need them to prepare them to meet you—I'm just saying!

4. "Why don't you want to be married?" Who said I did not want to be? Some days, I'm not sure if I do want to be married, but I can say this. I have gone through seasons being completely content with where I am in life, and then people ask, "Why don't you want to be married?" Most of the time, it comes from the same people that tell me I need to learn to be content with where I am. Go back to number 3. I can't win here!

At the end of the day, I think it's all about your intention. If your intention is pure and you have my best interest at heart, ask away. If you're asking just to ask, it can be really awkward for single people, especially when you want a different response than the one you get. All the single ladies, say *amen*!

> I say this as a concession, not as a command. But I wish everyone were single, just as I am. Yet each person has a special gift from God, of one kind or another.
>
> So I say to those who aren't married and to widows—it's better to stay unmarried, just as I am. But if they can't control themselves, they should go ahead and marry. It's better to marry than to burn with lust. (1 Corinthians 7:6–9)

Rebecca's Favorite Things

July 15, 2017

If someone asked you what some of your favorite things were, what would you say? I have lots of favorite things. It's only because I will basically do anything and everything with anybody as long as it's not illegal or won't get me in trouble somehow. I like adventure, so that's part of the reason why I like trying new things. Here are a few of my favorite things.

Mission trips. Why? I like to see different parts of the world and serve and experience God in ways I never would have in my own backyard. The world is so much bigger than we think, and if we are not careful, we will miss out on some amazing experiences.

Hugs. Why? Because when I have nothing to give you, I can always give you a hug. If it's someone that I really love and I have nothing else to give, then I can always say I love you and give them a big hug. Hugs are always free, and they're unlimited. And sometimes I am the one who needs the hug too.

Movie nights and game nights. Why? I am an only child. When you have board games that require more than one person, you never get to play them unless you have a group, so all of them are like new. I never get tired of them! I also like them because I like being around lots of people that like to have fun. Movie nights are just fun because it brings people together. And you have popcorn, so that makes it even better!

Playing with little kids. Why? I am a big kid, so I always have crazy things up my sleeve. And it gives me a chance to be the kid I never got to be.

Music. Why? I have always loved it, and it's *really* good for stress relief.

Smiling. Why? If someone sees you smile, then they will too. Smiles are contagious.

Roller coasters. Why? Because it brings out my crazy side.

Why am I sharing this with you? I want you to get to know me even from just reading this book. There is a whole lot more to my life than what you can see. These are just a few of my favorite things.

What are some of your favorite things? When is the last time you took some time to do something that you actually like to do for yourself?

> We have happy memories of the godly, but the name of a wicked person rots away. The wise are glad to be instructed, but babbling fools fall flat on their faces. People with integrity walk safely, but those who follow crooked paths will be exposed. (Proverbs 10:7–9)

Stuck in the Middle

July 30, 2017

I have never talked about this topic before. Here goes nothing! Unfortunately, this topic affects a lot of people, and it has become a common practice of everyday life. Before I say what the topic is, I want to say this to anyone who has gone through it: I'm sorry! I am going to talk about divorce. This is something nobody likes, but it is very real. And sometimes you have to deal with the hard stuff.

Divorce happens. Okay, we got that. It can either happen calmly, or it can be ugly. You could talk forever on the reasons why it happens. But we are not talking about the reasons why it happens. We are going to talk about the effects of it.

When divorce happens, it affects everyone. Even if you get remarried, you'll still wish somewhere deep down that it could have worked itself out, especially if you had kids with this person. If you had kids with your husband or wife, you are still forever tied to that person because of your child. How? Because your child, this one person, has your husband's or wife's DNA, and there is nothing you can do to change it. That child also still holds your husband's last name unless the child is adopted. As the husband or wife, you still have memories, good or bad, with this one person; and you also have hurt from this one person. Those kinds of things don't just go away. From a kid's perspective, no matter what the age they are, it looks like this: every other weekend, two birthdays, two Thanksgivings, two Easters, two churches, two Christmases, and two houses. Notice how I did not say *two homes*. There is a difference between a house and a home. When you make the choice to get divorced, your kids no longer have a home. They are stuck in the middle of two houses, living out of suitcases. You never thought about it that way, did you? Somebody is always going to fight over money, and your kids are going to feel like a prize to be won. They are always trying to make you happy even when it seems like they are not.

Kids don't have a voice in the matter until they are at a certain age, which is totally unfair because they get taken advantage of and run over by their own parents. Even if one parent or both get remarried and "move on" with their lives, the kids will still pay the price for their parents' marriage because they are always stuck in the middle. You may wonder how I know these things or even feel this way. My parents are divorced, and even though I know it was not my fault, I am still stuck in the middle. All these things you just read are only some of what I have experienced, and I don't want someone else to go through what I went through. The examples you set for your family matters whether they are good or bad!

> The Lord is close to the brokenhearted; he rescues those whose spirits are crushed. (Psalm 34:18)

> He heals the brokenhearted and bandages their wounds. (Psalm 147:3)

The Truth about You

August 13, 2017

We all sin. We all mess up on a daily basis, and we all know it. But something we don't always grasp is the truth about ourselves. We are always the first to cut ourselves down, then others do it too. Then it makes it even harder to believe the truth about you. God always thinks the opposite way of how we see ourselves. To him, we are worth more than the world could estimate. But to us, we let the world determine our worth. He sees lovely, and we see broken. We say guilty. He says forgiven. When we feel lonely, that is when He is the closest. God knows more about you than you know about yourself, but we are only going to know the truth of who we are when we are still, quiet, and peaceful even in the storm. I wish more than anything sometimes that I could hang on to those moments when I was peaceful and quiet. This is so much easier said than done. I would sleep so much better at night if I could truly grasp everything I just wrote. If only we could believe it. We get so caught up in all the wrong that we do that we forget to go back and look at the good things that we were actually created for. If we did, it would change the way we look at ourselves, and you would see the truth about yourself!

This is still a hard concept for me today. I don't think I will ever be able to fully grasp the way God looks at, sees, or thinks about me. That's what makes this so real and raw at the same time. It can be exciting for someone to know how God sees them, or it can be extremely emotional for someone who has never felt loved or has been hurt emotionally, physically, or manipulated.

Sometimes we simply forget how much God thinks about us. Maybe you have never been told, or you simply forgot. Either way, you need to know that God really does think about you.

He thought about you before you could think about him.

That is just how special you are to him!

> How precious are your thoughts about me, O God. They cannot be numbered! I can't even count them; they outnumber the grains of sand! And when I wake up, you are still with me! (Psalm 139:17–18)

I Have a Dream

September 3, 2017

I love to dream! I love to think about new ways to change the world. The really cool thing about dreaming is, if you believe it long enough and do everything in your power to make it happen, then your dreams just might come true. I have lived out some of my dreams, and it is the best feeling ever. Dreams start with a vision. What do you see when you think about the dreams that you have for yourself? Here's a better question. What do you have to do to live them out? I dream of changing the world one day at a time, and every day that I'm alive, I try to do one thing to change the world. I dream of living a legacy for people to look up to and of having a strong enough impact on the world that people will still talk about who I was long after I am not here anymore.

I have a dream that one day, the world will be different because I chose to look at it differently compared to everyone else. I pray that I leave a legacy that someone else wants to follow. I pray that God is so evident in my life that someone else wants to know where my smile comes from. More than anything, I hope that I accomplish all that God wants me to, not to glorify myself but to glorify Him. I have a dream that the world is just a little bit better because God chose to put me on the earth that He created.

This is a dream I have for myself, but it is also a vision I have for later. That's why I am doing something *now* to make it happen.

I am going to go back to my original questions. Please take the time to answer them honestly for yourself.

What do you see when you think about the dreams that you have for yourself, and what are you doing to live them out?

Your dreams for yourself play a part in who you become. Don't forget about that little kid who lives deep inside you! Kids dream about becoming anything, and they are not afraid.

Don't be afraid to dream!

> For God speaks again and again, though people do not recognize it. He speaks in dreams, in visions of the night, when deep sleep falls on people as they lie in their beds. He whispers in their ears and terrifies them with warnings. He makes them turn from doing wrong; he keeps them from pride. He protects them from the grave, from crossing over the river of death. (Job 33:14–18)

Bleed the Same

September 24, 2017

We live in a very connected world. Even when we are not connected, we are still connected. We are connected through social media, phones, email, instant messaging, and so much more. We are so connected to everything, and yet we are even more divided than ever. There is so much anger in the world over little things. We are so greedy that we are willing to take someone's life over what they have. We took God out of schools just because it might "offend" someone, and if a teacher even prays before school starts, she or he could be fired. Then we wonder why students fight with each other, and the anger that we already have grows into something we can't control. We look at each other and compare riches and glory while others are starving, naked, homeless, orphaned, abused, and sold like property. Even to this day, there are people that look at skin color and form an opinion of that person.

So how are we connected even with all these differences? Because we all bleed the same. We all have hurt. We all have needs. And we are all desperate for something. We are all looking for hope and love in the middle of the anger and rage. Even if you don't believe in God, you still put your hope in something that is just temporary and won't last. We are all made differently, but these things will stay the same. That is how we come together as one. If you ask me how to stay connected beyond your TV or computer, I would say this. Put your anger and selfishness aside because you are only adding to the divide if you don't. If you choose not to say anything, you are still saying something without saying anything.

You are saying, "I don't care about you. I only care about myself."

> Don't be selfish; don't try to impress others. Be humble, thinking of others as better than yourselves. (Philippians 2:3)

> For jealousy and selfishness are not God's kind of wisdom. Such things are earthly, unspiritual, and demonic. (James 3:15)

> There is no longer Jew or Gentile, slave or free, male and female. For you are all one in Christ Jesus. (Galatians 3:28)

The Good Fight

October 15, 2017

We all have battles in our lives. Sometimes we pick our battles, and then sometimes the battles choose us. We are not always given a choice of fighting in the battle. The choice we have is how we handle them. I have said that I have cerebral palsy. I did not choose to have cerebral palsy. Cerebral palsy chose me. The one choice I had was how I handled it. I could win, or I could lose. I have won and lost the same battle. I have had more battles than I can count, and it did not include cerebral palsy at all. And honestly, those battles seem to be harder. How do we win the battles in life? Have you ever noticed that for everything the world says about you, the Bible automatically has a comeback for it? Every war that we have ever had in history always had a strategy and a plan to defeat the enemy. Every army has someone to work on different ways to win each war they fight in. No battle ever has the same outcome. It is the same with the battles in our lives.

> ENEMY. Everyone said that I would never be able to do anything with my life.
> GOD'S WORD. Mark out a straight path for your feet so that those who are weak and lame will not fall but become strong [Hebrews 12:13].

I have now become a speaker, a missionary, and an author.

> ENEMY. Rebecca will never play sports.
> GOD'S WORD. Jesus looked at them intently and said, "Humanly speaking, it is impossible.

But with God everything is possible" [Matthew 19:26].

I have a black belt in karate, and I have played soccer.

> ENEMY. You have to have surgery, not just one but many. You will wear braces and be placed in a wheelchair.
>
> GOD'S WORD. I have told you all this so that you may have peace in me. Here on earth you will have many trials and sorrows. But take heart, because I have overcome the world. [John 16:33].

I have gone through more trials than I can say. I have had surgeries, braces, and wheelchairs, but that is nothing compared to some of the other things I have gone through. My body may look broken, but my heart is still whole.

> ENEMY. You will never have the strength to finish strong.
>
> GOD'S WORD. But those who trust in the Lord will find new strength. They will soar high on wings like eagles. They will run and not grow weary. They will walk and not faint [Isaiah 40:31].

How do I manage to keep fighting? Because I want to fight the good fight. How you stand at the beginning of a fight can determine how you stand at the end. Posture is everything! How did I make it this far? Because I already decided I was going to win before I even started the good fight.

If you had to create at battle plan for life, what would it look like?

Words Change the World

November 13, 2017

Have you ever thought about the words you read on a daily basis? We are reading even when we don't realize it. We read road signs, menus, books, Facebook posts, magazines… The list could go on forever. Think about the songs you hear. Somebody wrote the songs you hear in the car every day. What about TV shows? Every actress has a script to memorize. Somebody wrote every word they read. Think about what you're reading right now. I am writing every word. I have written two books, and hundreds of people are reading the words on the pages. The words I write will last longer than my life itself. I will still be making an impact on the world even when I'm dead.

I love reading the Bible. The writings in the Bible will live on for all eternity. The writers of the Bible are alive today because the Bible is God-breathed, and God lives forever! That's bone-chilling! I have said this before. One of my goals in life is to be more like Jesus. I am an author. Well, God is the author and the finisher. Therefore, I am more like him because I am an author and write for him. Words change the world when they are written. They can last forever.

> "But the word of the Lord remains forever." And that word is the Good News that was preached to you. (1 Peter 1:25)

> Your eternal word, O Lord, stands firm in heaven. (Psalm 119:89)

> Heaven and earth will pass away, but my words will never pass away. (Matthew 24:35)

God's Simple Blessings

December 9, 2017

I have amazing news! I have had another opportunity to release a new book! This is different from the last. My first book was an autobiography titled *Angel in Disguise*. My new book is a children's book titled *God's Simple Blessings*. What is this book about, and what was my motive for writing this book? *God's Simple Blessings* is special because it serves more than one purpose. This book teaches young children about the days of creation in the order that they happened in a fresh and easy way to remember. It also teaches children that they were created by God and that they also have the ability to learn how uniquely they are made. Does this book talk about salvation? Yes, most definitely! *God's Simple Blessings* explains salvation and the forgiveness Jesus gives us if we accept him into our lives. It also explains that when we accept Jesus into our lives, we will have a home in heaven when we die and eternal life.

When I wrote this book, it was coming from a very personal place in my life. Before I started writing this book, I was in a season of being extremely grateful for everything God had done in my life with my ministry, providing everything I needed for my first book. I was so thankful not only for my first book but for all the simple things in life. When I was younger, I never had big fancy things. I had things I enjoyed, but I did not have an overabundance of extra stuff. When I was little, iPads were nonexistent. I had a CD player, not an iPod. I had dolls I loved, board games, a bicycle, and coloring books. I am an only child, so I am very good at entertaining myself. My parents are also divorced, so I had a single mom. I was thankful for food, clothes, and a house to live in. That might sound irrelevant to most, but for me, it was a challenge. So I appreciate the small things a little bit more than most. Anything beyond that is a blessing.

If you look at the pages in *God's Simple Blessings*, every page thanks God for something, and it is written like a prayer because that is exactly what it is. I wanted to teach kids that they don't have to have the best of everything to get through life. I wanted to teach kids to be grateful for what they already have instead of begging for the next latest, greatest thing that comes out on the TV. That's my motive. *God's Simple Blessings* is twenty pages and has lots of colorful pictures. It covers all these things in one little book. Thank God for the simple little things in life. You are blessed without even knowing it!

> May the Lord bless you and protect you. May the Lord smile on you and be gracious to you. May the Lord show you his favor and give you his peace. (Numbers 6:24–26)

You, a Problem Solver?

February 17, 2018

We all have problems. Problems are a part of life. It's how you handle them that makes the difference. How you handle a problem can change the outcome you get when and if it gets resolved. I may step on your toes, but I must ask you this question. Are you a problem solver or a problem creator? Do you create a problem and expect other people to fix it for you while you do nothing to help resolve the problem? I like to help people solve their problems or at least make the problem not seem quite so overwhelming. I would like to think that I am more of a problem solver than a problem creator. In my life, I would think I have been both without realizing it. We all do it. We just don't like to admit it.

Problems are like fire. When we have problems, we have two options. Let's say that I am looking at a problem, and on the side of me, I am holding two buckets. One bucket has water in it, and the other has gasoline. I can either pour water on it and make the problem smaller or completely go away or pour gasoline on it and make it explode. Problems are only problems if we let the things we face become problems. Don't make your problems bigger than they really are! If you created the problem, at least help put out your own fire!

Depending on you, personally, you may be the person who helps resolve problems and stay calm, or you may be the one who makes mountains out of molehills without knowing it. I think we can all identify with both, depending on the situation.

With that being said, I am going to go back to my original questions.

Are you more of problem solver or problem creator?

Do you create problems and always expect other people fix the problems you made for yourself?

> Those who shut their ears to the cries of the
> poor will be ignored in their own time of need.
> (Proverbs 21:13)

I Can Only Imagine

March 12, 2018

I can only imagine what it will be like
When I walk by your side
I can only imagine what my eyes will see
When you face is before me
I can only imagine
I can only imagine

Surrounded by You glory
What will my heart feel?
Will I dance for you Jesus
Or in awe of You be still?
Will I stand in your presence
Or to my knees will I fall?
Will I sing hallelujah?
Will I be able to speak at all?
I can only imagine
I can only imagine

I can only imagine when that day comes
When I find myself standing in the Son
I can only imagine when all I would do is forever
Forever worship You
I can only imagine
I can only imagine

Surrounded by Your glory
What will my heart feel?

Will I dance for You, Jesus
Or in awe of you be still?
Will I stand in your presence
Or to my knees will I fall?
Will I sing hallelujah?
Will I be able to speak at all?
I can only imagine
I can only imagine (Bart Millard, "I Can Only
Imagine")

This song means something different to everyone. This song makes me smile because it gives me hope, but it also makes me cry too. I have heard it in so many places—funerals, radio, you name it, I have probably heard it there. Why am I writing about this song? Because even though I am here on earth, living and loving God, life is still hard sometimes, and I still think about heaven. I still think about what my life could be like without cerebral palsy and all the hardships that I have faced in life. I think about what it would be like standing next to the person who made me. I think about what it would be like to have my heart completely made whole instead of beautifully broken by the world or even people. There are things in life that hurt us, and I can't help but wonder what it is like to live in a world without the hurt and the struggle that comes with life. Life is beautiful because God created it. I have no questions about that. But it is also hard. I can't help but wonder about heaven too. I can only imagine holding the hand of the King. I can only imagine a world without tears. I can only imagine what Jesus would say to me. I can only imagine seeing all the ones I have missed. I can only imagine seeing the people that I love coming to heaven with me.

I can only imagine what it will be like
When I walk, by your side
I can only imagine what my eyes will see
When you face is before me
I can only imagine

The song "I Can Only Imagine" was written by Bart Millard. He is the lead singer in a Christian band called Mercy Me. It is one of the most popular songs in contemporary Christian music history. "I Can Only Imagine" has now become a major motion picture.

If you have never heard of this song until now, please look it up so that what I wrote will make sense to you. I also want you to hear it because this song tends to create a vision and a hope for anyone who really listens to it.

Where does your mind go to when you hear this song?

> The heavens proclaim the glory of God. The skies display his craftsmanship. Day after day they continue to speak; night after night they make him known. They speak without a sound or word; their voice is never heard. Yet their message has gone throughout the earth, and their words to all the world. (Psalm 19:4)

Passion into Purpose

April 29, 2018

Have you ever wondered why you do the things you do? I have, and to be honest, sometimes I'm not exactly sure why I do some of the things I do. Have you ever done something and then turn around and say, "Why did I do that?" not because you regret what you did but because you really don't know why you did that one thing? I was once asked this question during a question-and-answer session: "Why did you want to become a missionary?" To be honest, I wasn't sure how to answer that question at first. Why did I become a missionary? I love helping people and being able to give back to them. I never would have thought those two things would turn me into a missionary. After I thought about this question, here was my answer. Keep in mind that I am sitting in front of a live audience.

"If I look back on my life, I can see how God always kept His hand on my life. If I look back, all throughout the Bible, I can see that Jesus came to serve and not to be served. If I claim to be a Christian, which means to be Christlike, that means that everything I say and do should look like Jesus. Therefore, I came to serve and not to be served, just like he did." That was my answer to this question. This is how my passion turned into my purpose. I will also say this. I am not perfect, and I will never claim to be. Jesus did not ask us to be perfect. He just asked you to be willing. I got where I am today because I was willing, not because I am perfect.

Why do you do the things you do in life?

> For even the Son of Man came not to be
> served but to serve others and to give his life as a
> ransom for many. (Matthew 20:28)

Expectations

July 22, 2018

I have a question for you. What are your expectations? What are your expectations for yourself and for other people? What do you expect from others? I am going to throw myself in the pot for a minute. If you have heard me speak or have read any of my books or blogs, you should know by now that I am not afraid of being human. I think, sometimes, people have an impression that everything is always okay and that I am always happy. That can be a good thing, and it can be a bad thing.

I may be a speaker, a writer, and a missionary, but that doesn't take away the reality of what life can be like sometimes. Over time, I have become very good at hiding my emotions. This is not something I wanted to be good at, but in a lot of ways, I was forced to hide how I really feel. What really bothers me is the fact that when I finally felt like I could open up to someone I trusted, the only thing they would ever say was, "You will be fine," or, "You will be okay." Translation, people. Here is what that really means: "You're Rebecca. You will figure it out because you can get through anything!" If I am taking the time to open up to you, number 1, that means there is a piece of me that trusts you. That is a big deal for me! Number 2, if I am trying to talk to you face-to-face about something and I am the one who comes to you first, that means something is really bothering me. Everything is not fine. I'm not okay, and I cannot do life all by myself. I am just like you! I laugh and smile, but when I get really tired and frustrated, I cry. I once heard a pastor say this in the middle of his sermon: "It's okay not to be okay." That is so true!

What are your expectations of people?

If you know me personally and are surprised by what I wrote, then your expectations for me are too high. If you have never met me, then you just met someone who never holds herself too high for others to reach.

> Confess your sins to each other and pray for each other so that you may be healed. The earnest prayer of a righteous person has great power and produces wonderful results. (James 5:16)

The Life of a Substitute Teacher

July 30, 2018

I have written about many different parts of my life, and over the past year, I have started yet another section of my life that is still fairly new to me. I have two blog topics, one called "The Life of a Missionary" and another titled "The Life of a Babysitter." Today I am going to write about the life of a substitute teacher. Yes! I am also a substitute teacher! Let me first say that I never saw this coming, and I never saw myself ever doing this! It is one of those things that fell into my lap, and even though I am still new at this, it has been one of the best things I ever did to help myself. How did I get here if I never saw this coming? Let's just say that teachers make teachers. I was highly encouraged, and somebody cared enough about me to not let my hidden talent go to waste. Needless to say, here I am, writing about my life as a substitute teacher and what I have experienced so far.

You get phone calls at 5:00 AM, and when that happens, the principal gets to hear what you really sound like in the morning. No one in their right mind is awake then, which means you won't remember the conversation. Being a substitute teacher is the only job you will have where you can be five different people in one day. You don't always get the memos until after or when the event is taking place, so you always bring food on the wrong day or not at all. When the kids ask for help, they expect you to know everything they are learning about even though you only spend one day in their classroom and have no idea what the lesson was that got them to where they are. You read chapter books starting from the middle because you were not there for the beginning or the end. So you have no clue what is going on. You can almost guarantee that there will be a fire drill on the one day that you have the hardest class in the whole building.

All the kids know your name, and if they really love you being in their classroom, they will fight over you in the middle of the hallway (best feeling ever!). You get some amazing new artwork to hang on your wall because they love to draw for you! I get at least five hundred hugs a day because they know I want to take them all home with me. You go to birthday parties, graduations, and award ceremonies because you love to see them smile back at you. It is even more awesome when parents come up to you and randomly say, "My kids talk about you all the time!"

This is just some of what I have experienced so far. The life of a substitute teacher is full of surprises, and you really never know what your day is going to hold. But somehow, it is the one piece of my puzzle that was missing, and it all fits together.

> Let the message about Christ, in all its richness, fill your lives. Teach and counsel each other with all the wisdom he gives. Sing psalms and hymns and spiritual songs to God with thankful hearts. (Colossians 3:16)

Jesus in Disguise

August 26, 2018

If you saw Jesus, would you be able to recognize him? When someone hears the name Jesus, they may feel a number of ways. Some may think about love, grace, peace, etc. while others feel anger, rage, and hatred. Why? Because so many people think that Jesus only goes to the nice and clean places. They think that Jesus would only show up in churches, retreats, revivals, or mission trips. They never think that Jesus would meet them exactly where they are—in the darkest part or place of their life. What if Jesus walked into a jail cell or hospital room or walked on a sidewalk, homeless and hungry? Would you be able to recognize him or judge him for how He looked? What if Jesus came to jail through a pastor or even another inmate? What if Jesus worked through a doctor or nurse to heal someone? Would you notice or thank the doctor without thanking God first? If Jesus were naked, hungry, and homeless, would you provide for him or just pass him by? After all, He does ask us to take care of those who have less than us. Jesus is the only perfect man that ever lived on earth. He went to places no one else would go. He was humble and kind. He used the weak to lead the strong. He lives in the ones you least expect and goes to the places you never thought of going. You never know when you might meet Jesus in disguise.

Would you recognize him?

Parable of the Good Samaritan

Jesus replied with a story: "A Jewish man was traveling from Jerusalem down to Jericho, and he was attacked by bandits. They stripped him of his clothes, beat him up, and left him half dead beside the road.

"By chance a priest came along. But when he saw the man lying there, he crossed to the other side of the road and passed him by. A Temple assistant walked over and looked at him lying there, but he also passed by on the other side.

"Then a despised Samaritan came along, and when he saw the man, he felt compassion for him. Going over to him, the Samaritan soothed his wounds with olive oil and wine and bandaged them. Then he put the man on his own donkey and took him to an inn, where he took care of him. The next day he handed the innkeeper two silver coins, telling him, 'Take care of this man. If his bill runs higher than this, I'll pay you the next time I'm here.'

"Now, which of these three would you say was a neighbor to the man who was attacked by bandits?" Jesus asked.

The man replied, "The one who showed him mercy."

Then Jesus said, "Yes, now go and do the same." (Luke 10:25–37)

Please Don't Forget

July 13, 2019

I'm not sure what it is about people, but it seems that when people learn that you have wisdom and a lot of life experience, they will automatically hold you up to a different standard in life. The longer I am in ministry the more I feel this way. Take a minute and just hear me out.

I absolutely love what I do! I love serving God, helping others, being an ear when people need it, and being a person that someone can lean on at any time. I'm not saying it's wrong that people hold me to a different standard, but I am saying that there is a lot of pressure on me that you may not see. I am grateful for the respect and trust that people have in me, but there is something you need to understand. I'm a human being, not a superhero. Please don't forget that I still have doubts and uncertainties. Please don't forget that I still have bad days and hard times. Please don't forget I still get frustrated and angry and that I cry when things hurt me. Please don't forget that I may not have an answer to your problem. Please don't forget that I still make mistakes and that I still need the grace of God just as much as you do. Please don't forget that I may be the one who needs help from time to time. Please don't forget that I may need someone with an ear for listening and a shoulder to cry on when life is rough. Please don't forget that I need people in my life I can trust just like you. Most importantly, please don't forget I can't always be strong because I am 100 percent human just like you. I will never be so high that you can't reach me or so low that you can't see me.

Please just be yourself around me so I can be myself around you.

I remember writing this blog like it was yesterday. Even as I think about it now, I can still remember how much this reflected my state of mind. My emotions were high, and I was running on empty. When I wrote this blog entry, I was at Grady Memorial Hospital in Atlanta, Georgia, with my grandparents. They were in a car accident, and I wrote this one day while I was sitting in the ICU wing of the hospital. My eighty-six-year-old grandma was in a fight for her life. She was there for a month, which means I was too. When I wrote this, I was exhausted and uncertain of what was coming next. I had a ton of support from others, but I also felt isolated from the world. I needed the people in my life who could handle seeing me at my worst. I needed the ones who could hold me up when I could not hold myself up anymore, and I definitely did not need to be alone for a long period of time. I didn't want to hear "Stay positive" or "It's going to be okay" because it did not look okay at all, and no one knew what the outcome was going to be at the time. I wrote "Please Don't Forget" because some had forgotten that I am 100 percent human and not a superhero. Sometimes I needed the listening ear, that shoulder to sleep on, and the ones who could be strong for me when I could not be. This was a reminder to others that I am just like them and that I am not excluded from hard times and the ups and downs that come with life.

"Please Don't Forget" was the last blog I wrote. As you are finishing this, I want you to know that I don't expect you to always be strong, happy, or your own version of perfect. I don't want you to feel like you ever have to be a superhero around me. I want you to be you around me because if you are yourself around me, then I can be myself around you. I am all human, and so are you, good or bad. I do not think of myself as "better" than the next person.

What I get to do is love people exactly where they are.

Please don't forget that!

> So now I am giving you a new commandment: Love each other. Just as I have loved you, you should love each other. Your love for one another will prove to the world that you are my disciples. (John 13:34–35)

Special Acknowledgment

Writing books is a long process. The kind of books I write always come from a deep place in my heart and from lots of life experiences. Putting these two things together can sometimes cause me to go back to memories I don't always like or cry tears I didn't even know I still had. Even though I laugh a lot and smile, life is still hard. At times, my life in this world can be a lot for me to process. With that being said, I have someone I would like you to meet. I would like for you to meet my dear friend Sonya. I met her in 2019. She is a Christian counselor. Sonya spends her time caring for others' mental, emotional, spiritual, and physical health. She also looks after the ones who have been hurt by trauma from major life events. Sonya is very down-to-earth, loving, and trustworthy. She has a beautiful personality with a touch of "momma bear" hug inside her.

How do I know her?

I am one of the people she graciously looks after. Sonya helps me take care of myself so I can continue to help others. I have had my own trauma and life events that have affected my health overall. But I still manage to lead people to Jesus in the process. Sonya is also the one who inspired me to write the book you just finished reading. One day, while I was sitting with her, I was talking about wanting to write another book about a side of my life's story that no one had public knowledge of. Both of us decided that is was not time for that yet. I gave Sonya the website for my blog page, and she started reading. Sonya gave me the idea of turning my blog into a book, and in the summer of 2020, I "picked up the pen" once again to make the book you are holding in your hand. If it were not for God using Sonya to get me to this point, the book would have never happened.

Sonya has taught me two very important things.

Number 1, it is okay to take time to care for yourself.

Number 2, it's okay to have someone help you along the way.

If you don't know how to do these things, you not only are not helping yourself, but you are putting yourself in a place where you can't help anyone else. Your health from every angle matters.

I want to thank Sonya for all of her love, knowledge, and wonderful understanding of all of my life's issues. God placed her in my life for a lot of reasons, and writing this book was definitely one of those.

May God bless you in all that you do.

Love, Rebecca

About the Author

Rebecca Leatherwood lives by a passionate belief that, in life, it is important to be willing but not perfect. Having overcome the challenge of being born with cerebral palsy, Rebecca's childhood was not like most. When she was nine years old, she met Jesus and willingly surrendered her life to service unto him and others. At nineteen years old, Rebecca published her first autobiography, *Angel in Disguise*. One year later, she would author her first children's book, *God's Simple Blessings*. Over the years, she has become involved in missions, and in 2021, she will celebrate the tenth anniversary of becoming a public speaker. When she has a free moment, Rebecca enjoys spending quality time with family and friends and traveling to the beach.

Printed in the USA
CPSIA information can be obtained
at www.ICGtesting.com
LVHW051555121223
765933LV00049B/674

9 781685 174460